Food for Thought
Letters to Friends

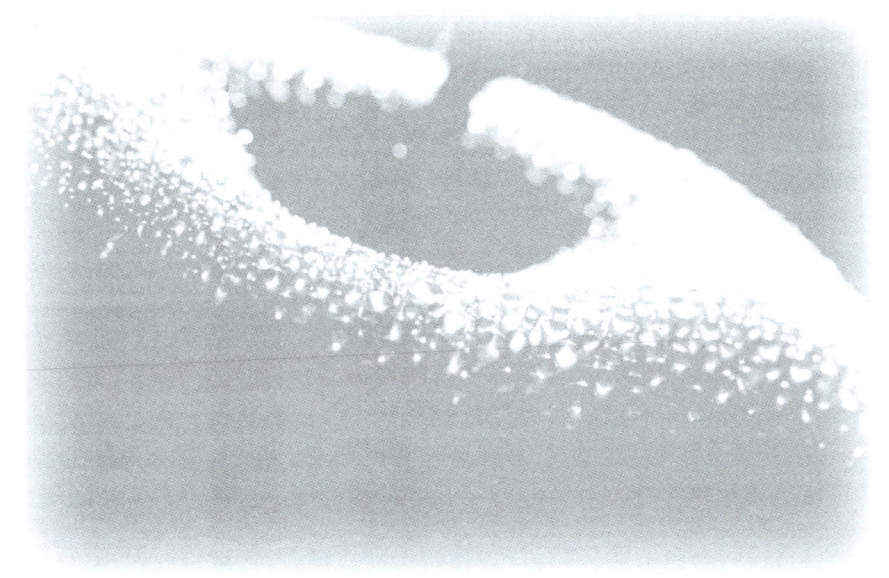

By Alec McPherson

Copyright © 2010

Published in the United States by
Insight Publishing Company
707 West Main Street, Suite 5
Sevierville, TN 37862
800-987-7771
www.insightpublishing.com

All rights reserved. No part of this book may be reproduced in any form or by any means without prior written permission from the publisher except for brief quotations embodied in critical essay, article, or review. These articles and/or reviews must state the correct title and contributing authors of this book by name.

ISBN-978-1-60013-566-8
10 9 8 7 6 5 4 3 2 1

Dedication

I would like to dedicate this book to all my mentors—there were so many—my spouse, bicycling and running friends, my children, parents, teachers, brothers-in-law, my pastors during my youth and as an adult, co-workers, and, yes, even a boss or two.

Probably the most influential were the following, but not in any special order:

My mother. Everyone says this, but she taught me to hustle, be organized, and use numbers. She had a spirit that never said it couldn't be done.

My father who taught me compassion for everyone, no matter what his or her status in life was. He also gave me the infamous list of "Things to Do" every day.

Rev. Frank Webb, who was the pastor of Vergennes United Methodist Church when I was a senior in high school. I maybe should have listened to him more then. When he retired at 86 for the final time, he offered me his robe and his file cabinet full of sermons.

Kenneth E. Smith, my brother-in-law, who subconsciously persuaded me to be an engineer because I respected him so much. He brought his toolbox to the farm every weekend to repair things. I watched him in awe.

My boss at Hale Pump in Conshohocken, Pennsylvania, Ray Hartenstine. He taught me why it was important to be honest. He said we are not smart enough to tell little white lies; eventually we will get caught.

My wife and family who have taught me you aren't the boss at home, so you had better be persuasive!

There are so many others at all the places where I worked and played. Chevy in Flint, Hale Pump in Conshohocken, Allied Signal in St. Joe, Clarksville, Pemco Die Casting in Bridgeman, and now at Symmetry in New Hampshire and Warsaw. Each of these folks taught me more than I ever taught them by a multiple. And from each group I grew a little more.

Strangely, my growth opportunities usually, but not always, came from adversity. And of course there were the pastors at all my local churches, as Karen and I moved, and all the personal friends (we have moved umpteen times).

The "quietest influencers" have been my running partners and biking friends. It is truly amazing how close you grow to a running and or biking associate.

Many of my pastors and co-workers were the inspiration for these little one-page "sermonettes" or "Food for Thought" I have written.

Table of Contents

CHAPTER 1

    ATTITUDE   1

        It is a Wonderful Life   1

        It is Your Health   4

        Pollyanna   6

        Hey Coach   8

        "What a Beautiful Morning"   10

CHAPTER 2

    COACHING THE BIG GAME   13

        Change   15

        Some People Don't Like Lou   17

        Share in Success   18

        The Best People   19

CHAPTER 3

    THE JOURNEY TO CHANGE THE WORLD   21

        Life was Simpler then   23

        Do Something Different   26

        Some Call it Luck!   27

CHAPTER 4

    LISTENING   31

        Just the Facts!   33

        Pyramids   34

        Share our Information!!   35

CHAPTER 5

COACH, TEACHER, AND STUDENT — 37
    Let Me Offend You — 39
    How Goes the Job Hunting? — 41

CHAPTER 6

EASY IN THE GOOD TIMES — 43
    Popular Sport — 45
    It is Great to be Alive! — 46
    Eternity — 48
    To Dream — 50

CHAPTER 7

TENACITY — 51
    Success — 52
    Give until it Heals — 53
    You Are Your Mirror — 56
    Coaches — 57
    Focus — 58
    Who to Blame — 60
    Jump in and Paddle — 61
    Food for Thought — 64

CHAPTER 8

PRAYER — 67
    Pride — 69
    Trust — 70
    Things are Seldom as We Perceive — 71
    Hello, I am a Christian — 73
    Be Profound — 74
    Empathy — 76

Rules That We Teach	77

CHAPTER 9

BE PROUD 79

Big Picture	81
Do You Remember Your First Real Job?	82
No Man is an Island	84
Clean it up for us	85
Walk to Emmaus	87
TROOP	88

CHAPTER 10

GOALS FOR THE NEW YEAR 91

Blue Sky	93
We are Healers	95
10 Best Days of Your Life	96
Visionary	97
Power of Prayer	99
Good guys and bad guys	101
Results count!	102

Introduction

I wish I could remember when I wrote my first sermonette. I may find it as I do my research. However, I may have written a few at Hale in the late '70s, but they became much more prolific when I was at Bendix in St. Joseph in the early '80s, which would later become Allied Signal.

I was struggling as a manager. I was younger than almost all of my employees, and a lot less experienced. But, I was hungry, energetic, and had a ton of ideas.

I wanted to help my employees improve faster and faster, so that as a team we could be the best. I had read tons of books and taken dozens of management classes in my master's programs, but none seemed to be right 100 percent of the time.

I eventually came up with "Theory Z" modified. Everyone you work with and who works for you has a different hot button and needs to be managed accordingly. Always remember the real goals, don't sweat the small stuff, and stay focused on the big. Always come back to taking care of your people and your customer—the money will come. Of course, part of taking care of your people is teaching them how to take care of the money.

Early in my career at GM (probably in 1972), I was part of a few folks writing the early statistical process control standards for machine capability. A lot of data collection and analysis! It was the forerunner of Six Sigma and SPC! In the early '80s I went to Japan and studied Employee Teams. I heard Eli Goldratt speak live in the mid '80s; it was an awakening. Why can't we put all of these together (Eli, lean, Six Sigma, SPC, and Employee Teams)?

However, it wasn't until I was at Clarksville when I had the real opportunity to try all these crazy ideas. Strangely, they worked; but it was a new plant with no tradition, so Noe Gaytan, Jim Fox, Dick Brisson, and I had our chance of a lifetime to experiment. We experimented and had great success and great fun.

I tried my ideas and management style at St. Joseph Allied Signal plant, but was not extremely successful. It was an old plant with a ton of tradition, and it was like trying to steer a barge with a rowboat. The same thing at Pemco—I continued to try my philosophical communications and training with moderate success. The difference was that at Pemco, Terry Allen actually encouraged me to refine my management style using more Eli Goldratt and more Six Sigma.

It now seems to all make sense at Polyvac and Othy, divisions of Symmetry medical.

If you have the right people, with good, basic values and good work ethic, you can have a tremendous journey

Alec

CHAPTER 1

ATTITUDE

It is a Wonderful Life

If you have not seen them before, I call them food for thought. Their intent is to give you my thoughts on how we can work together better, have more fun, and enjoy our job and our lives a little more fully.

We spend a lot of time at the plant; it should be friendly, productive, and rewarding. It should be a place of learning and trust where we strive to grow as a company and as individuals. We need to work smarter, work harder, help each other, train, learn, and grow.

Four events occurred this weekend that inspired me to think about the whole improvement process. I don't know if I can tie them together but I will try.

My wife and I saw the movie, *It's A Wonderful Life,* on television Saturday night. Have you seen it? It is a story about a down-home young man named George Bailey (Jimmy Stewart), who never makes it to college, takes over his dad's savings and loan business, sends his younger brother to college, and is always helping other people. George gets down on himself for being a failure twenty years later when there is a financial crisis at the savings and loan. His guardian angel, Clarence (Henry Travers), shows him what the world would be like if he had never been born and that is when George sees the good in his past actions.

Sometimes we don't realize how good we have it, relative to the rest of the world. Sometimes we don't realize how good we have it at our own plant and in our own personal job.

The second event happened when I was driving somewhere in Warsaw. On some church marquee I saw the sermon line, "Be thankful in all things." This is tough! How can we be thankful for pain and suffering, for broken bones, or car accidents? Maybe we need to look at just the smaller things. How can we be thankful for everything we have? I can think of how a plane crash is good as long as my family was not involved in it. I guess I am thankful when they weren't.

The third event occurred when I was reading an article about goals and incentives. It suggested that the greatest incentives are from within and the most lasting are when we personally help others.

Fourth, I read an article about "What makes people happy" in *USA Today*. Surprise! It is not money—it is more about friends and your support group. It is family and the people around you. It is keeping busy with daily activities and it is the ability to forgive easily.

Okay, how can I tie this together? We really have it pretty good in the United States of America, and at our businesses. We can be thankful for jobs and friends where we work. Sometimes we don't realize how much of an impact we can have by helping others. We can be thankful for our customers and our industry. Many industries are not and have not been making any profits for several years. We can be thankful we work for a small company where you actually know and can talk to the CEO. We have a wonderful place to work and keep active, and a friendly group to work with. We should be happy. We can take all this to the next level if we focus on sharing skills, training each other, supporting each other, sharing best practices, and helping each other learn how to do our jobs better communicating. We can all be happier and more productive when we help each other.

I usually am very positive and happy with my life. I have a great family and a ton of close personal friends; but I hate to admit when I am wrong! I can be very defensive when someone points out that I am doing something in a less than efficient manner. It upsets me that I did not think of it. Usually after I think about it, I want to try the new idea. It if works better than the old way I was doing it, I like it even more. I also am very forgiving; I usually forgive many times. First, I don't want to worry about whose fault it was and I don't want to worry about remembering who screwed up. It is just easier to forgive and forget.

Take fifteen minutes a day and think about how you can do your job better. Look at how your neighbors are doing their jobs and share best practices. Forgive them when they make a mistake, help them learn from it. Share with them your best practice.

It is Your Health

As I sit here with one of the worst colds I have had in years, I am trying to write an article titled "How to live a healthy lifestyle." When our kids were still at home, I would tell them that wellness is all about attitude, exercise, and eating right. Whenever I would get a cold, it was their favorite line to remind me of my three healthy suggestions.

I read a book three or four years ago called *The 100 Simple Secrets of Successful People* by David Niven! He has written more than a dozen self-help books. Niven stated that, ". . . researchers have found that those whose careers continue to have momentum are 53 percent more likely to engage in healthy life habits than those whose careers are stalled." That doesn't say "100 percent." It doesn't say "promotions." It says *"career momentum."* He does suggest that people who exercise moderately and eat reasonably have more fulfilling careers. Health is a three-legged stool of exercise, attitude, and consuming healthy products!

Exercise can be jogging, walking, gardening, or even golfing. Eating right can be balance and moderation in everything. I have a good friend who runs seven days a week covering more than thirty miles. When he was seventy years old, he had quadruple bypass surgery. He had been eating a Whopper and fries for lunch for twenty years. Exercise alone is not enough to let you abuse your body by consuming tons of fat-saturated super-sized foods.

Attitude is all in your mind. Stress also plays a big part in your health; exercise helps control stress. Alcohol, caffeine, and smoking do not help with stress. You only think that they help stress. A good book and/or meditation help reduce stress in just minutes.

Why do we want you to live a healthy lifestyle?

You will be a more productive employee over the long-term.

To help control rising health care costs so we can maintain our compensation plans.

The real reason that you should change to a healthy lifestyle is for you and your family. Do it for them. Do it for you!

Most of the company's medical costs are statistically long-term lifestyle habits such as not having exercised for years, eating a super-sized burger and fries every day, smoking for years, driving without seatbelts, drinking and driving, extreme overweight for years, and so on. We have concluded that the only way to control medical costs in the future is for us to encourage you to live a healthier lifestyle.

Moderation in everything keeps the mind and body healthy. Start by getting a little exercise, eating moderately, and reading a good book! It is all about statistics. If you exercise, eat right, have a positive attitude, and don't abuse your body, the probability is that you will have a healthier, longer life.

Pollyanna

I know my vision may be a little overly optimistic but if we dream, it might as well be in color and have a happy ending.

I have long had the following vision for all companies where I have worked:

Our employees are happy, safe, secure, learning new skills, enriched, empowered, and contributing. They are fairly paid employees who enjoy their jobs and have time to enjoy their personal lives. We benchmark other companies, generally promote from within, hire the best, and retain our employees. Employees are proud of where they work. We aren't the highest paid and we don't have the best benefits, but we are better than average. We are the best place to work.

Our customers tell us that we are their supplier of choice, not because of price but because of quality, delivery, and service. We listen to their needs and can be trusted.

We have the best equipment and a clean, efficient, fast, lean shop floor that produces custom products that we ship faster (less dock-to-dock time) and are of better quality than those of our competitors. There would be very little scrap and rework—less than 1 or 2 percent—and very seldom a remake. The floors and machines are clean and orderly with very little in process material. Dock-to-dock time for repeat orders is less than two or three weeks (first operation to RTS). Almost every indicator is predictable with very little variation.

We have a plethora of our own patents and standard designs that our customers are demanding. Most of our orders are blankets.

Okay, enough—as long as we are all heading in this direction. We can't, or at least we don't, want to go back to the fifties where employees were never involved. Quality and the customer were seldom listened to. We can't go back. We must make small steps every day toward our vision.

How do we attain our vision?

We must have a thirst for new knowledge, benchmark others, read, and listen.

Knowing is growing and we must take that knowledge and understand its application for us. We must experiment and implement what is right for us. The trick is discerning what is useful and what is not right for us. We can try to predict the impact on the vision we have above. If we predict it is good and there is little downside risk (and if it should fail can we easily reverse it), we should try it. If the opportunity is low and it can't be reversed, we may wish to study further or maybe not try it at all. Sometimes the opportunity is high and the risk is high; then we may choose to pilot the change.

We must have the courage to try new ideas and to change.

We must have metrics for our goals and focus on the single improvement that will give us the most the fastest, for the least investment.

FOOD FOR THOUGHT

Hey Coach

Frank Milne and I were talking about coaching his son's soccer team. Then that weekend, my son and I were talking about his high school soccer team that he coaches. It made me think about how coaching is like business and business is like coaching. In both business and sports, we need identifiable goals. There should be some stretch in setting the goals, but with a lot of work and a little luck they should be obtainable. For example, a good goal may be to finish the Boston Marathon again, whereas a poor goal for me would be to win the Boston Marathon. We need to set a goal. Let's say last season we had seven wins and ten losses and that our goal for this year is to have a winning season. It is the same for business—we need to set a goal or have a mission statement about where we want to be a year from now or three years from now.

I know that I am a little compulsive, but I set goals every year for physical fitness, spiritual and mental growth, my financial savings plan, my family, my work, and to learn something new each year. I believe it gives balance to my life.

Now we need to define how!

We need to do an analysis of our talents and weaknesses. With that analysis we must decide if we can accomplish our goal best with brains, strength, speed, team spirit, or a blend of all these. How often have you seen a team of great players have a losing season? It was probably because they were so weak in one of the other areas that they never gelled as a team. Look at the Notre Dame football team a few years ago compared to the prior year. They had the same players as prior years with a new coach and several new assistant coaches; they are undefeated midway through the season. What changed? Mostly spirit and maybe some smarter planning!

I think there are four key elements in winning soccer games; business success is similar.

Brains: Play smarter—have better planning, better analysis of the competition, better equipment, better training and drills, and better assistant coaches. Know your costs, price accordingly, measure skills, and work on improving individual skills.

Strength: Work harder and faster, have longer practices, lift weights, arrive at practice on time, never miss practice, have one person run two machines, and use very efficient practices.

Speed: Hold running drills, lift weights to increase speed, manufacturing cells, Smed, and reduce lead times.

Spirit: Work as a team, have a can-do attitude, and when you are losing or have a bad day, don't give up.

I personally think the greatest of these is spirit or attitude.

Have you heard the story about the high school graduation where the students were not allowed to pray or mention the word "God" in the graduation ceremony? The valedictorian planned a strategic sneeze at the end of their remarks and all the seniors said, "God bless you"!

Did you hear about Leonid Brezhnev's wife? When he died in Communist Russia in 1982 (Christianity was still forbidden), just before they closed the casket, she pulled a cross from her pocket and laid it on his chest and closed the casket.

Spirit and attitude are what win games. Of course, this is true only if you have worked hard, trained hard, and have good coaches. Working together with a positive can-do attitude is what wins games. Always looking for a way to improve as a team to give your team a little edge is what wins the next game!

What a Beautiful Morning

You may not have known, but I am a gospel music aficionado (translate that, crazy zealous nut). I love the major keys that are positive and bright. I don't like many of the minor keys and dissonant cords that sound depressing. I took two years of piano but I promptly forgot everything.

Some of my favorites are "Morning has Broken," "What a Beautiful Morning," and many others. I like them more for the words than the key.

We have a choice every day when we get up to be optimistic and thankful or be pessimistic and negative.

The *Trading Places* television show is an offshoot of the BBC version and is quite unique. Your neighbors come in and, with some direction, totally remodel one of your rooms or your garden. Afterward you get to see what you asked for. You also have the chance to remodel one of your neighbor's rooms. Sometimes you get more than you expected by trading places and sometimes the neighbors cut the legs off grandma's antique dining room table, cut a hole in the center, and make it a planter. As my grandfather used to say, "Be careful what you wish for."

In my career I have worked in some really nasty manufacturing plants that were really hot and filthy. I have worked in two different sand foundries that often were more than 120 degrees in the summer with dust so thick you could not see from one end of the plant to the other. I also worked at a cast iron CNC and machine shop where the air was so full of iron dust and coolant oil that my shirts had turned rust red by the end of the day. A die cast where I worked was so steamy that mold and fuzz grew on the walls.

In 1966, I started working as an hourly forklift driver, brake press operator, and paint line person. I worked for some really nasty supervisors, yelling tyrants, and crazy people. In those jobs, and a few others, I worked for minimum wage and received no benefits. Overall I have worked in many wonderful environments and had many more good supervisors than bad ones.

So everything is relative. We need to be thankful for what we have and continuously remind ourselves that, yes, we could be doing a lot worse.

As we work to improve quality and cost for our customers, we can improve our wages and benefits for our employees. If we don't improve our quality, costs, and delivery, we cannot improve wages and benefits.

As you probably know, I like to make lists. You can try it. Make a list of the ten things that really matter to you in your life and at work. Think about the things that you think will matter ten or twenty years from now when you look back. Safety, health, and family should be high on your list. Be thankful for what you have and make a long-term plan to improve the others.

Be thankful for the things we have at our company. Have a beautiful morning for yourself and your fellow employees. Think about how we can make this a better place to work for yourself and your fellow employees ten years from now. As business grows, so can our employees.

Sing a song, whistle a tune, and be thankful. Plan for improvement.

FOOD FOR THOUGHT

CHAPTER 2

COACHING THE BIG GAME

Part 1

While my two sons were in junior high school and high school, I coached high school soccer for what seemed like eight years, but was actually only a few years. Having only played four or five years of college intramural soccer without a formal soccer coach, I really did not know much about soccer strategy. So, when I became a coach, I read several soccer coaching books; they all stressed technique.

Since I had played defense, I coached and stressed defensive techniques. My teams had the lowest number of goals scored against them in the league, but we lost almost every game because we did not score many goals.

After that coaching experience, I changed my coaching and management style. I now believe in giving the team tools to achieve goals, keep statistics, and work on attitude and communications, while recruiting the best players and hiring great assistant coaches to teach technique.

Part 2

Have you ever noticed how one play in a football game early in a season can make a difference for the whole year? A few years ago, when the Big Ten quarterback fumbled late in the game against a rival, his team lost the game. The whole season went downhill, along with the quarterback's entire career.

Another Big Ten team missed a field goal attempt against its rival at the end of the first half that year, when the coaches thought it was fourth down—it was actually third down. The field goal was blocked and the rival team ran it back for a touchdown.

When mistakes happen, the players can get down on themselves and lose their self-confidence. Players get away from the fundamentals, and start taking too many unnecessary risks. They quit working as hard in practice, and they start blaming other players, and so on.

It can happen in a company, it can happen to you and me. We can't let one fumble change us so much that we quit wanting to carry the ball. Sure, we have to understand if we made a mistake and correct it, but we can't stop playing the game.

Part 3

In summary, often employees know more about how to make parts than I do. Often others know more about making parts than you do. But, it is up to us as managers to communicate, motivate, and, when workers make a mistake, re-motivate. Our goals are simple—keep employees and customers happy now and in the future; make money now and in the future. If we do these two things, we will have lots of job security.

We don't need to teach our seasoned employees technique. We need to give them the metric and let their positive attitudes complete the task. We need to hire and retain excellent assistant coaches, and help the whole team build confidence.

Change

Manufacturing is a continuous search for improvement. We can never stop and we must always anticipate the future.

"If you keep doing what you have always done, you will probably get what you always got!"—Mark Twain.

Even though we have done well, we have not done well in past down turns. We want a new, different, and more favorable result when business slows.

୰   ୰   ୰

It is interesting for me to watch what is happening with Ford and GM, since I started my career at GM. I think GM lost its customer and employee focus, and was preoccupied with short-term, traditional financial metrics. They downsized, de-proliferated, commonized, cut engineering, cut models, dropped Olds, etc. They seemed to focus on short-term money, and short-term Union contracts.

How can we avoid those issues? We must know our global environment, our customers' pain and hot buttons, our customers' goals, and our competitors' strengths and weaknesses. We must continuously search for improving our position in the environment so that our numbers stay strong and our employees secure.

So, for sixty seconds, stop what are you doing and think about what you are doing and ask:
- Will it help our position in the environment in our customers' eyes?
- Will it strengthen our global position?
- Will it reduce our lead times and improve our quality?

FOOD FOR THOUGHT

- Will it improve our employees' skills?

Love change, anticipate change, and seek it first.

If you keep doing what you have always done, you will probably get what you always got.

Some People Don't Like Lou

What do Muhammad Ali, Elvis, Ronald Reagan, and you have in common?

Most people like you and me, think you are the greatest, but lest you get a big head, there are quite a few who don't like you or me and don't agree with either of us.

Hopefully, it is neither your boss nor your customers who dislike you. In his book, *The 7 Habits of Highly Effective People,* Stephen Covey talks about friendship bank accounts. You make favorable deposits and unfavorable withdrawals with your relationships. If your friendship bank account per Stephen Covey falls below zero, it can be a problem for your project support.

However, life and work are not a popularity contest. It is really about your objectives. You need to have a metric and measure your success via the metric. Yes, even life at home has metrics—safety, food, shelter, savings, etc. Usually the metric is easier to obtain and improve if you have people and family support.

The bottom line is that you must please yourself; your metric and your attitude is how well you accomplish that metric. It is wonderful to have friends, but it is better to accomplish your metric *and* have friends. Your attitude is all in your own mind. Be proactive, positive, and self-motivated on your metric.

In his book, *The 7 Habits,* Stephen Covey talks about how to motivate your people with a positive bank account. You don't have to be nice and agree 100 percent of the time with your friends, but you need to deposit more good deeds than bad notes to maintain a positive relationship. The bottom line is that your attitude is up to you!

Share in Success

In my opinion, success in business is all about helping each other. We help each other when we share ideas, skills, and when we assist each other.

So, how can I help you today?

First, assist and serve: I have a spare hour or two; what job can I assist you with that you either don't want to do or don't have time to do? Please understand that my skills are limited, but I am willing.

Second, share: I had a success yesterday, thanks to you. I appreciate your showing how to fix my problem.

Success is all about sharing and support, serving each other, and being a wild and crazy team bent on continual improvement and customer satisfaction.

The Best People

Some of the best employees I have ever had work for me were employees someone else thought should be let go. I do not know what this means other than maybe sometimes it is the job, sometimes the employee versus boss chemistry, sometimes the boss, sometimes the employee motivation, or sometimes just timing. I have also been let go several times in my career. I know there were things I could have done differently, but most of the time it was just either chemistry or the wrong place at the wrong time. Of course, I always liked to think it was the boss just making a mistake (LOL). Judge your people for yourself. Don't always take others' word for it.

In summary, we, as managers have a huge impact on what our people produce. This is a product of the power of positive expectation, the willingness to tolerate and even encourage diversity. The power of listening and involving leads to more motivated employees, and creates a better work environment for our employees.

What do we want: on-time delivery or dollars? Obviously, we want both. If I had to state a number of priorities in order, it would be as follows:

Involve, encourage, enrich, listen, train, and fairly compensate our employees.
- Customer satisfaction numbers.
- Service.
- Quality.
- On-time Delivery.

The numbers, EBITDA dollars, Cash Dollars, Ship dollars, Order dollars in that order—percent does not count.

Of course we want all three.

FOOD FOR THOUGHT

If we empower and train our people and understand the metrics in goals two and three, we will have a winner. Let your people make the daily decisions that improve the numbers.

CHAPTER 3

THE JOURNEY TO CHANGE THE WORLD

"No Journey is too great if you find what you seek" (from the 1988 movie *Coming to America,* screenplay by David Sheffield and Barry W. Blaustein).

Sometimes I wonder how much we will remember about what we did this month twenty years from now. My guess is the details will mostly be blurred. We may remember something if we got a new job, or had a new grandchild, but most of the details will be lost.

What will be remembered fifty years from now when most of us are gone? Unless you are a Heisman trophy winner or president of the United States, very little! So, I look at every opportunity as four hundred mousetraps with four hundred ping-pong balls. With every action there is a reaction. What will be remembered isn't the action but the reaction multiplied by four hundred every day. Every little change you make causes many others in a chain reaction.

There is a church hymn, "Take Now My Voice," by Douglas Nolan. The final line is "Change the world through me." Most of us as individuals have very little impact on the world. As a team helping each other and sharing ideas, we start a ping-pong ball mania. One of my favorite sayings is, "If you keep doing what we have always done, you will get what you always got." So if what you are doing is good, keep doing it. If not, change is needed.

All change has obstacles. Every result has a cause; every change has an effect.

Life and business is like a chess game. Before we make the first move, we have several options to consider. And our opponent or competition has several options after each of our moves. We must consider each of his or her potential moves and think about our next move, and several moves ahead. We must be prepared for all outcomes of our actions and have an alternative action or reaction planned consistent with the risk and severity. Adverse reactions teach us to anticipate unplanned events while errors teach us to look for the whys and fix the cause. Competition teaches us to look for giant leaps in improvement, or the competition will leave us behind.

For example a company announces in the news that thousands of employees being laid off and filing for bankruptcy. We need to change and change faster. Ideas give others ideas. Ideas and improvement multiplies, giving speed to improvement and training processes. We need a thousand little ways to do things better and faster.

Life was Simpler then

I was listening to the country song "Remember When" and I started to remember simpler times.

October 1963 was a normal day. I had a dollar and change in my pocket. Gas was ten cents a gallon at the Zephyr station and recycled oil was a nickel for my 1953 flathead Ford Customline. I bought the car that summer from L J McCall and paid $150. I got $75 from Dad and $75 from my 4-H earnings. The $75 from Dad was for the 51 Buick with a blown up engine (I won't say which older brother did the dirty deed).

That summer someone hit my '53 Ford in the parking lot and gave me $75 to not report it. I repaired it myself for $6 with junkyard parts. I just had it repaired when another person hit me in Ada in the left rear bumper and gave me $45 to not report it. I repaired it for $3 with junkyard parts. Life's simple pleasures!! So, between Dad and me, we paid $11 for that wonderful car.

It was fall and all the apples were picked. I was sixteen and didn't have a steady girlfriend that week. I wanted one, but had no takers. I wasn't on the first string in football, wrestling, or any sport, so no pressure. I usually had lunch at Christensen's drug store with my best friends from school. I probably only had one or two best friends but I had lots of good friends. Mom would give me money for lunch but I would take two apples and use the lunch money for gas for that 1953 Ford. Those days when I carried my lunch, I would walk to Hahn's Hardware or Murphy's Metal Shop and bother them while they worked. I loved the hardware store and I loved watching Mr. Murphy the tinsmith.

I didn't have a savings account and did not read the WSJ. The war in Vietnam was just a military exercise with advisers sent by JFK after the French pulled out and it was never in the paper. The only magazine that I received was *Popular Mechanics*, a Christmas gift. I read it cover to cover every month.

My only boss was my dad and when I goofed up, he never fired me. He would just give me another list of things to do that Saturday. It was a steady job with outstanding job security—and no pay. LOL. When my dad got mad at me, he got over it in minutes. He must have been very tolerant and very forgiving because I goofed up a lot.

I seldom watched television. There were better things to do: Go to Lowell to the high school football game and have a burger at Rosy's or Kaiser's Kitchen. Go to Ty's and lift weights. The 4-H square dances were great and everyone danced, without asking. The church choir sang hymns and I sang them a hundred times. The pianist always played our parts and there was no fancy accompaniment.

I listened to the AM radio a lot— classical, regular music, and the new stuff, rock 'n' roll. Those were the only choices. There were only two or three stations on the black-and-white television and the shows were not very good.

I only had one pair of dress shoes and an old pair of tennis shoes and one pair of barn boots. I had two pair of barn jeans, and two pair of school slacks and maybe four or five school shirts. I had one sport coat and two really thin neckties. It was easy to dress for special events. I did have lots of winter coats that were hand-me-downs from my older brother and bigger cousins.

I still had a full head of wavy hair and never knew about dry skin in the winters. I never remember heartburn, even if I ate a whole cherry pie or a whole coconut pie that Mom had made. I did not know what bunions were. And I only had to shave every three or four days, probably not that often. I seemed to only need five or six hours of sleep—unless I could sneak in a nap under a tree between farm chores. I ate a lot of red meat, bacon, and gallons of whole milk.

There was no such thing as planning for a getaway vacation when you milked cows twice a day, seven days a week. It was a wonderful schedule.

I don't know what my favorite thing is about those days. Some special things were family and friends, church, 4-H, and the 4-H fair in August.

My favorite time—no one knows. When I would get home from the football game at 11 PM, I would park my '53 Ford and walk along the path back to the apple orchard. The sky was so clear. The crisp fall air and the stars were so very bright with no city lights from Grand Rapids. I would sing loud—any song. What a wonderful life.

It still is a wonderful life. It just is not as simple today.

Have a grape day!

Do Something Different

In the October Communications meetings, I had numerous really good questions regarding how we could improve. I loved the questions. It gave me a warm feeling that you understood and cared.

I think there are a lot of initiatives in place to improve Customer Delivery, Quality, and Profits in every unit and every department. A few of the initiatives are:

Six Sigma black belt and green belt projects
5S
Vantage schedule and shop floor data in 2005
New machines
New employees
Employee Machinist Certification

But we need more! The real issue is "What can I do differently?" (a team expression). "What can YOU and I do differently?"

Keep doing the good things and continually look for ways to improve speed and quality.

There are always obstacles but the truly successful find a way. They are tenacious, persistent, never give up, find alternatives, compromise, and discover new paths in their struggle to improve. We never want to sacrifice the intended use of a product. We never want a product to fail in a surgeon's hands. We want to find ways to make products faster and easier.

So, what can you and I do differently today? I have a list of things that I can work on; I need to prioritize them. You can do the same.

"Think blue sky, out of the box. What can I do differently?"

Some Call it Luck!

She was just in the right place at the right time. Dad, it was not my fault! The Bank made an error in my checking account of $2 and now I am overdrawn. I am bored: I have lived here for three years and don't have any friends in this little hick town. There is nothing to do in this town. It was an accident! I hate that line. Okay, I don't believe in luck.

I do believe in statistics. And I do believe in relationships and networking because twenty-two years ago I was let go from my job and did not know anyone. I began to build a network when I suddenly realized I already had a network—I just did not know it because I was not keeping in touch. For twenty years I have tried to maintain a huge network of friends and associates, professional friends, church friends, family, head hunters, fellow runners and bikers, barbers, college friends, and so on.

Back then people used the telephone and wrote letters to keep in touch. Wow, today it is so easy with e-mail. Many years ago, when I was released by Allied Signal (now Honeywell), I had developed an active list of two hundred to three hundred friends and associates throughout the previous fifteen years. In addition, I had a list of almost more than one hundred executive search people.

In the ensuing four months, I had seventy job interviews with thirty-three companies. Ninety-seven percent of these interviews came from my personal network. Two job interviews came from my barber. Dozens came from fellow Honeywell employees. Very few interviews came from newspaper ads or executive search companies.

Strangely, I used one of my closest network people to be my mentor in my job search. Even stranger, my mentor helped me prepare for half of these job interviews and was my sounding board when I was down. But the strangest, was when that mentor offered me a job. Networking is everything,

Rule #1 is to build a network. Everyone is a potential referral for you or for you to help him or her.
Rule #2 is to never ask for a job—ask for advice.
Rule #3 is to keep your network current every month, preferably with a phone call or face-to-face, but minimally with an e-mail.

Networking gets you a job, gets you a promotion, gets your project completed on time, and lets you have more fun. Many years ago, when business was really poor, my mentor had to let me go and bought out my share of the business. I had my network and within days, I had several job offers. However, I thought I wanted to start my own business and I needed my network to help me get started. The first network person I called, I asked for advice. He said, "Why don't you sell my company for me?"

Networks are great (maybe a little homemade luck).

Starting your own business is all networking and making sure everyone knows what you are doing. Promotions and friendship are all networking. I worked on expanding my network. When I called on a network friend I ask him or her to give me a name or go to lunch with me and one or two of friends in that person's network. In a few months I had had seventy lunches, breakfasts, or business contacts with network people. I had added almost one hundred new people to join my network. None of this now four-hundred-member network was an executive search person.

I could not keep up with my growing network. What a great problem. Example: I joined Business Networks International. The network is based on the principle, "Givers Gain," a great slogan coined by founder, Dr. Ivan Misner. I immediately had a network of thirty people and each of them had a network of twenty more;

my network grew by six hundred people. Now, strangely, the first of August, while making a consulting sales cold-call to my prior Honeywell boss to push my operations excellence package, before I ever started, he offered me a job. It was not luck. It may be statistics but networking is everything.

Rule #1: Build networks.
Rule #2: Ask for advice, and try to take it.
Rule #3: Spend a lot of face time with your network; at least send e-mails.
Rule #4: Add just a few retained executive search people to your network.
Rule #5: Grow your network.

The most important rule of networking is "Givers Gain." Give to your network. When someone in your network needs help on his or her project, or a referral, a reference, or a job search, give that person a hand.

Thanks—you are on my network list.

Food for Thought

CHAPTER 4

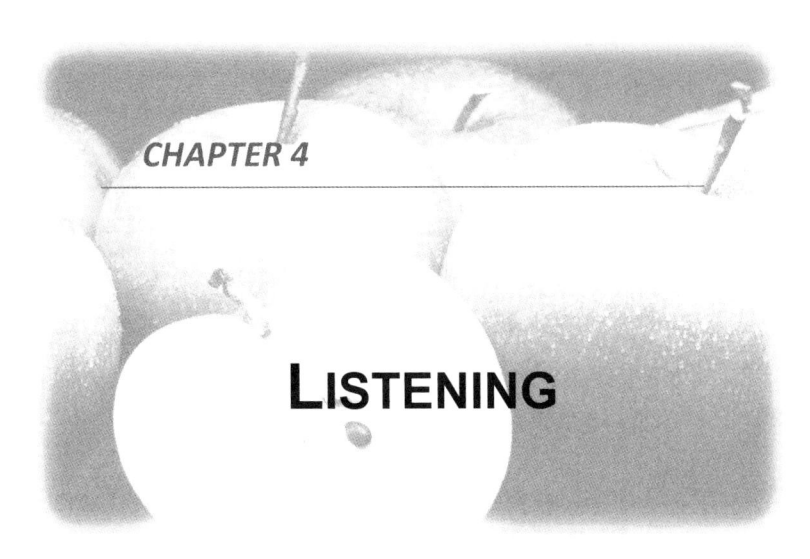

LISTENING

I am not convinced that we listen to each other. Yes, you and I do not listen to each other very well. Or, if we do listen, I am concerned that we don't remember or we just don't take any action. Our priorities are not in harmony (i.e., we aren't in the same boat, let alone all rowing in the same direction).

Examples:

I ask that you send someone to the communications meetings to write down questions. No one showed. Small issue, but an indication.

Attendance at 10:30 AM Monday and Friday meeting is poor. When you are absent, many of you fail to send a representative.

We published a schedule for the communications meetings over a week ago, yet the room was not set up and ready at the needed time.

I asked a month or two ago that chairs be ordered for the new conference room so we would not have to borrow chairs from the training room. Chairs either have not been ordered or not received yet.

We list things to do at our leadership team meetings, but little activity takes place week to week.

We are now almost halfway through the year, and you and your direct reports all have tasks on your bonus plan. I see some evidence that you are working on them, but I see some that are past due and no activity.

We get feedback that we don't have raw material for a blanket item for a customer. The very definition of a blanket is to have three months of raw material on hand at all times.

We are still past due on jobs and we are slow. The only unit that has very little past due is department C, and they have lots of Excel special tracking sheets that still lets things slip through, like item 7.

Okay, so I trust that you get the point. We need to change how you manage your business and pay more attention to priorities and detail. This means all of us, including myself.

We must be more rigorous in maintaining a TTD list with priorities. YOU must have a daily written TTD list. You can't just be a firefighter.

We must be more rigorous in taking notes. Start carrying your palm pilot or your Franklin planner or just a notebook. Look into the new BlackBerry phone PDA.

We must be more rigorous in following up with our direct reports and insure they have a TTD list and a priority that agrees with yours. You must set up a formal follow-up system, either on the Outlook Tasks, notes, or Franklin planner.

You need to review your priorities and the priorities of your direct reports weekly.

You need to learn how to use Outlook scheduling.

We must quit letting the little detail be forgotten. So, dig out your Palm, buy an electronic organizer, a BlackBerry, a Franklin planner, or at least a notebook.

Just the facts!

Share our information! Usually we make decisions based on our biases and on the data we have available. I believe almost all employees try to make the correct decisions based on data, input, experiences, values, etc. Sometimes we are tempted not to listen to the customer or corporate leadership because we think we know better based on our data and experiences. And sometimes we do have information that the others do not, which may change the decision options.

The problem arises when we don't all have the same data. We must constantly share the all the data or all the information. If we all have the same data, most Western civilization people will always come to the same conclusion.

Problems arise when the customer or corporate leadership cannot share all the information and data (just the facts). Sometimes this data or information is confidential and cannot be shared. In those few instances we can ask some questions, but we must take it on faith that they are making the right decisions.

In all other cases, we need to be better at sharing facts and then we will all make similar decisions.

Pyramids

I have been thinking about pyramids.

You have heard of pyramid sales programs. If you are on the top, it is great but only the people toward the top of the pyramid really gain.

There is also the book by Joe Girard titled, *How to Sell Anything to Anybody*. He says that all of us have twenty really close friends we can sell to or talk into something.

Are you with me?

Now, there is a third idea—"share your bread and fishes" (i.e., knowledge is power). If you have a skill or knowledge no one else possesses, you have power.

Now let's combine these three principles. Pyramids, twenty close friends, and share your knowledge. If you share your knowledge with your twenty closest friends, you have multiplied your power and knowledge and that of your twenty closest friends. However, if all of your twenty closest friends share their skill and knowledge with you and their twenty closest friends, we have a multiple of four hundred.

Just sharing your bread and fishes will increase your knowledge and power by four hundred.

Share our information!

Usually we make decisions based on our biases and on the data we have available. I believe almost all employees try to make the correct decisions based on data, input, experiences, values, and more.

Sometimes we are tempted to not listen to the customer or corporate leadership because we think we know better based on our data and experiences. Sometimes we do have information that the others do not which may change the decision options.

The problem arises when we don't all have the same data. We must constantly share the all the data or all the information. If we all have the same data, most Western civilization people will always come to the same conclusion.

Problems arise when the customer or corporate leadership cannot share all the information and same data (just the facts). Sometimes this data or information is confidential and cannot be shared. In those few instances we can ask some questions but we must take it on faith that they are making the right decisions.

In all other cases we need to be better at sharing facts and then we will all make similar decisions.

CHAPTER 5

COACH, TEACHER, AND STUDENT

At one time or another, even during the same day, we can be the teacher, the coach or the student. I have borrowed this line from a friend, Jim Fox.

Are you a knock-knock joke fan? Rev. David Neuen used several in his sermon on Sunday:

Knock knock. Who's there? Boo. Boo Who? No need to cry, I won't tell many jokes.

Knock knock. Who's there? Orange. Orange who? Orange you glad I am not a comedian.

I love this type of joke! It must be that my sense of humor went bad someplace. In fact, my favorite joke of all time is the following:

Knock knock. Who's there? Abraham. Abraham who? Abraham Lincoln.

Smiles and laughter!!! Ask me to tell it. It is all in the delivery. And the more you tell it, the better it gets. Now you know why I don't tell more jokes.

Knock-knock jokes bring us to doors! We have an open door policy at our company. That means we endeavor to be open and honest with our communications with all employees. Doors are usually meant to be two-way—communications, trust, and honesty is to our mutual benefit. We share information with each other in an effort to have continual improvement. Suggestions often lead to solutions or at a minimum they lead to other ideas, which lead to solutions.

All of us at times are teacher, coach, and student, depending on the question. Questions sometimes have risks, but often have huge rewards. Sharing knowledge should be our greatest strength. Sometimes you are asking the question; sometimes you are answering the question. Sharing knowledge, asking and answering questions, and coaching each other will make our company a better place to work and more financially secure. Of course we can all be students and take advantage of our tuition and books refund program.

And a few quotes from my last little epistle, sent to me by Max Elder; they seem appropriate for today:

"Any coward can fight a battle when he's sure of winning; but give me the man who has the pluck to fight when he's sure of losing"—George Eliot.

"To reach a port we must sail, sometimes with the wind and sometimes against it. But we must not drift or lie at anchor"—Oliver Wendell Holmes

"It is quite possible to work without results, but never will there be results without work"—Anonymous.

"It's easier to prepare and prevent, than to repair and repent. The time to repair the roof is when the sun is shining"—John F. Kennedy.

Let Me Offend You

I once heard and liked the statement, "Try never to offend anyone unintentionally." Wow, think about it! This could mean that one tries to offend people or it could mean that a person tries not to offend.

Teamwork might suggest that we discuss data and we do not discuss fault, or we do not try to hurt or offend someone verbally. Sometimes even jokes offend. IT DOES MEAN WE SEEK RESOLUTION AND ROOT CAUSE!

Sometimes we tend to remember the worst or the best, but we seldom remember the average. We need to remember the little things that people do. In his *7 Habits* book, Stephen Covey says that we all have a bank account and we make deposits and withdrawals based on the good or bad things we say and do to others. Good things are deposits and the objective is to have a positive bank balance. Those little things add up and they have a way of accruing interest. The more good things you do for others the more those people good things do for others, and it eventually comes full circle. We should be sharing best practices, sharing ideas, and training each other for the benefit of the whole. We can't wait for someone else to help someone. Sometimes we must take action.

Best brings out the best!

Competition is very tough. We compete daily for orders based on quality, delivery (lead time), and price. Often price and lead times are the deciding factors. Competition is coming from new areas of the world. We must continuously improve and we must dramatically improve our lead times, our quality, and our customer delight. Since we don't want to be in a price war, we must be in a service, quality, and delivery war. To be the best we must benchmark and train each other in the best processes for quality and lead times.

FOOD FOR THOUGHT

I don't want to offend any of you unintentionally, but we need to improve faster. Don't blame anyone. Just seek to improve. Our vision is more than 99.9 percent in customer quality, more than 99 percent for on-time delivery and less than half the lead times of our competitor.

Have a grape day!

How Goes the Job Hunting?

I was reading or listening to a television show on my trip to the U.K. about personality profiles of managers. One of the discussions was about entrepreneurs and the personality traits of successful entrepreneurs and successful senior execs.

On many of my job interviews during the last thirty years and all those blasted Myers-Briggs Type Indicator assessments, I was trying to outsmart my interviewer. Often the only result was that I outsmarted myself. I answered questions based on what I thought my personality profile should be or what I wanted it to be. I also took a Mensa test about the same time and found out that I am not that smart. In fact, I think I am getting dumber as I get older!

I also think that some of my personality profiles have changed during the last thirty-five years that I have been working. Hopefully I am becoming more tolerant and a better listener. I was thinking that you need to decide what your real personality profile is. How has that made you successful? Sell it. Maybe you have decided the same, in which case you are ahead of me.

I used to tell to headhunters that I was a team player, a people-person, data-driven, results-oriented, used tough love, and so on. The article suggested that successful entrepreneurs are driven, never accept failure, obsessive, rule-breakers (can't accept paradigms), and risk-takers who think out of the box and love change. I thought, "Wow, that is almost me." I want to be a people-person, a team leader, and not a micro manager. But I think I am an obsessive-compulsive data person, a huge risk-taker, who loves change almost to the point of loving change for the sake of change. I hate rules, policies, procedures, and the corporate mandates that slow change (almost to the point of cheating on corporate procedures or rewriting them, but not to the point of breaking any "major" laws), and I love to be around hard-working people; I can't tolerate slackers. I am driven, almost anal about finding a way to win. I love contests and incentives almost to a passion.

The article also suggested that successful entrepreneurs have huge egos, are extremely self-confident, terrible team players and love seventy-hour weeks. None of which fit my profile (LOL). I don't like to work seventy-hour weeks anymore. I know my average is only about fifty-five to sixty.

I sometimes think that headhunters want to hear that you are a mean SOB who gets results. Companies say they want people-people, team players, etc., but they really want results at almost any cost. So, if you have not come to the same conclusion in your interviews, sell yourself as you really are, not as you think you should be.

CHAPTER 6

EASY IN THE GOOD TIMES

It is easy to be motivated and have a sense of urgency in "Good Times."

It is easier to be positive when things go right.

It is difficult to anticipate "things gone wrong" and put preventive controls in place.

It is difficult to be an optimist and work hard when things go wrong.

It is easier to run efficiently when you can find all the tools, fixtures, parts, routings, gages, and so on.

It is difficult when you can't find the tools, fixtures, gages, and etc. We need to think about why we can't find them and put in place corrective actions so we can find them in 5 seconds or less. Now is the time to refuel, to energize, blue sky, brainstorm, and think about how to make operations a better world. We need to prepare ourselves mentally by training and emotionally by being positive.

We need to prioritize all our brainstorm ideas so we don't duplicate effort and work first on the biggest, quickest improvements that get us the most new orders.

Be Prepared

Play chess and plan your next three or four moves, but have alternatives that depend on the customers' and competitors' moves

My favorite parable is "Spike and the Fox."

Spike was Snoopy's cousin in the *Peanuts* cartoon.

Spike decides to go on a foxhunt with all his bigger, faster dog friends. But after a short period he is left far behind, and it starts to rain; he gets cold and hungry. When Spike thinks all is lost, the fox comes along and shows Spike the way home.

So, sometimes it is the person you least expect who can help you. Often, we can learn from the least expected source. So, help each other.

Our whole objective is to improve all aspects of customer satisfaction in order to obtain more business.

Popular Sport

Business, politics, and religion all have so much in common. If you don't have popular support (or a great majority of support) for your programs, you will have a battle. In most wars (Revolutionary, Civil, Spanish, WWI, Korea, Vietnam, and Iraq there was a small majority—maybe not even a majority—who approved. Religious reformations are another example. It was a minority who led to change. Look at the Japanese industrial revolution. A few copied Juran and Deming. Now it is the world's mantra.

My point is that in our business, a few want to change and are hoping for improvement. Often a large number of people fight for the status quo. If you are the change agent, it is very helpful to have a coalition and to have everyone involved. Just because no one follows does not mean it is wrong. Change is not easy but as leaders you need to have a very positive attitude and think about the opportunity for improvement. Things seldom improve if you don't change. In fact, if you don't change, you will slide back into failure.

Great leaders want a majority to support them but leadership and decisions are not a popularity contest. So, support the initiatives, involve your people, listen to the obstacles, address the obstacles, and make the decision that the data tells you is in the best interest of your people and the customer. I am a student of the Pygmalion effect—if you believe, it will happen.

It is Great to be Alive!

We have so many opportunities. And luck is often what we make it. If you saw the article in the paper some time ago, luck is often recognizing opportunities and having the will to take action. Change and risk can be our friend. We "all" need to think about our next great breakthrough.

I know you may be having a great year, but we need to be thinking about the next quarter and next year. Life is all about change. We must continue to improve and change. Our number one focus must continue to be customer quality and on-time delivery. Breakthrough thinking should focus on ideas that can dramatically improve on-time delivery.

A few Sundays ago, our pastor told a story (If I listened correctly) about an Indian who found an eagle's egg that had fallen from the nest. When he looked up, he saw that the nest had been destroyed. He walked a little farther and found a prairie chicken nest and put the eagle egg in with the other eggs. The eagle egg hatched and the hatchling grew up thinking it was a prairie chicken. One day, the young eagle looked up in the sky and saw a magnificent bird flying above and asked the older prairie chicken what that was. The older prairie chicken said that is an eagle. You can never be an eagle. You are and always will be a prairie chicken.

I am not saying we are prairie chickens, but I am saying we can be eagles—if we choose. We must dare to dream!

My vision for our future!

My first vision is continuous improvement in everything we do—a 25 percent year throughout-the-year improvement until we are at or better than the benchmark, better than the competition by a significant margin, and our customers' best supplier.

25 percent year throughout-the-year improvement in customer quality, on-time delivery, GP dollars, safety, lead-time, profit, inventory, etc.

Safety is probably zero LWIR, and less than 1.0 TCIR.
Lead-time is less than the freight time from China.
Our customer quality is at or exceeds 99.5 percent for the yearly average. And is better next year.
Profit is better than planned.
Delivery will be the tough one; it is so volume-dependent. But with planning and working smarter, our long-term vision must be better than 98 percent.

My second vision is that we are having fun and we involve all people. We are training people for career advancement, if that is their goal, and if not, we are training them to do their current job better. Hire and retain the best. Have a good, a well thought-out succession plan.

We have a great incentive system. Enhance it a little with money and perks, little monthly incentives to increase awareness, involvement, and fun. Involve more people in decision-making and extra activities.

My third vision is that our housekeeping will be impeccable and that all our employees will be extremely proud of where they work. Our plant will be a visual showplace for customer visits and that we present a visual perception of excellence from the moment a visitor drives up to our plant and until they complete their tour. This may mean a little rearrangement and/or an addition.

My fourth vision is that we will work closely with our partners and that they will feel part of us and we will feel part of them. And that we can learn each others' best practices.

Thus the vision is that we want to continuously improve the vital few: on-time delivery, customer quality, profit dollars (not percent), and employee fun quotient.

Eternity

Section One

A friend of mine was in Elder-Beerman the other day looking for a men's cologne. He asked the young lady at the counter what was the most popular brand. She replied that Eternity was her best-seller. He then asked for a sample of Eternity.

How appropriate and what a great story.

Why do we seek eternity? Why are we so afraid of death?

For me it is the unknown. I don't know what dinner will be either, but I know there will be something. If we are truly Christians, we know that eternity will be something. I am guessing that we fear death because we will no longer be with our friends. But if we are truly Christians and our friends are also Christians, we will eventually be with our friends for eternity. It can't be that we are afraid of what Heaven will be like. The bottom line is that we really are not 100 percent sure that Heaven exists and that we are going there. The result is that some of us work extremely hard at staying healthy so we can live long lives. I wonder if we work as hard at being Christians? If we are really strong Christians and we truly believe in Heaven, why not go there now?

Two reasons:

- I believe it is our job while we are here to convince others that Heaven is real and show them how to get there.

- I believe we don't choose when we leave this Earth and we should not take our own life.

As an avid runner since 1981 (now reformed), I think I was addicted. Today I am probably almost as addicted to bicycling and chocolate. My goal now is to be as addicted to being a Christian as I was to running. I want to enjoy praying as much as I enjoy a hot fudge sundae.

If Christianity is the Opium of the masses, I want to be addicted. And I am very confident that if I ever want to become un-addicted the devil will take me back.

Section Two
I must be honest—I am afraid of death, yet I profess to be a Christian. I am pretty good at disguising my fears but they are there. There were times when I thought my life was threatened and I prayed in earnest. And I must admit there are times that I have not prayed when I should have. My best prayers that helped me the most were the simplest. I just prayed that the Lord would handle my problems and that His will be done. Lord, please take my burdens. Handle this for me. It worked—I could sleep at night.

I assume it is common to fear death, but it is how we deal with that fear that matters. Easier said than done!

To Dream

My grandfather, Grandpa Gordon Frost, used to say that we could do anything and accomplish anything we really wanted to do. He also said that we had all the time we wanted to do the things we really wanted to do. What he did not explain was the "really wanted to do" part. To dream of what we really want to do! To dream is to have a vision of a better (you fill in the blank). To accomplish a dream requires change. Thus, we must anticipate change, expect change, want change, and even love change. We need to think "blue sky" about how it could be better.

We must not just change for the sake of change alone. We must not change randomly. We must manage change and focus on changing the one or two things that will get us the most the fastest. Once we focus together, we can set our one mission, one set of objectives, one set of priorities, and move consistently toward that change.

By working together, communicating, helping each other, trusting, and treating each other with respect, it will be so much easier and so much faster to complete projects.

One mission is to have one vision, one set of objectives, one set of action plans, one priority list, and work together on the same list. We can be even greater by working together on the same list of goals. Total alignment!

Dare to dream with me!

Sometimes when the road is blocked with adversity, we do our best dreaming!

P.S. Grandpa Gordon lived to age eighty-six. He was a great peach farmer and a great fisherman (at least his fish stories were great).

CHAPTER 7

TENACITY

It seems sometimes that some things—even great ideas—take forever to implement. Have you noticed that? But, if you give up, if you don't have the persistence to continue to push and ask, it will never happen. Keep asking, keep collecting data, keep looking at the issue from other perspectives, minimize it, magnify it, and keep asking Why? Eventually, the light bulb on the porch will come on.

So, that is why I like Swiss cheese. With enough holes poked in a problem (i.e., cheese), eventually the problem will be solved and the cheese gone. If you have a really big task, poke holes in it until it is an easy task. That is why I like Six Sigma. While collecting data, analysis of that data often lets the solution jump out at you. Sometimes you need to collect the data at several detail levels you never imagined (e.g., by machine, by fixture, by fixture location, by operator, by shift, by hour, etc.).

So, if you have a problem that you can't solve, work on it a little piece at a time. Collect the facts and the data and review all that you know. The solution will come.

Success

Years ago, I read an article about the "Fundamentals of Success in Manufacturing." I was digging through my old files for my notes. I found them and this is a summary of my interpretation. I believe very strongly in these fundamentals:

- Take care of your people
- Health, Safety, Housekeeping, and Environmental
- Meetings
- Metrics
- Capacity planning

Take care of your people: Have a good training program, and testing. Pay them well, share the incentives, encourage goal-sharing, formally communicate the issues, involve them, empower your people, hire the best, retain the best, biggest raises to the best.

Health, Safety, Housekeeping, and Environmental: Meet or exceed all laws and regulations. Have a continual improvement process, do audits, have a steering team for Health, Safety, Housekeeping, and Environmental.

Meetings: Have a daily meeting with key people to review yesterday and today regarding schedule, quality, generation, scrap, issues. Have a weekly leadership TTD, priority, and major issues meetings. Have monthly business management and strategy meetings and review the metrics.

Metrics: Define your metrics. Have a continual improvement process such as management by facts sheets (e.g., net profit, cash, safety, customer satisfaction, etc.).

Capacity planning: Know your capacity. Know your constraints. Plan and price accordingly.

Give until it Heals

My son gave a sermon a few years ago titled, "Give until it Heals,"

It started me thinking—why can't work be more fun? I know. A strange connection!

My mother's advice to me when I went off to college was that 10 percent of the people love their jobs, 80 percent just do them, and 10 percent really hate their jobs. Mom said, "Find a job that you really love and the pay will take care of itself." Well, so why can't we all be in the 10 percent who really love our job? Mary Poppins that I am, I believe we can. It is a matter of perspective, assuming we are in the right industry and right occupation.

Some thoughts!

- Work until it is fun instead of work until you are tired.
- Work happily and smarter.
- Work for the joy of it.
- Celebrate your job, say good things, and think good things.
- Think about what you are trying to accomplish and who you are trying to help.

Our job is to give to others. It transcends above making things. Our higher job is "making life better for others" through reconstructive and trauma surgery. So, what makes something fun other than food, friends, chocolate, games, and giving? Oops! Maybe *that is* the key—working with friends, games, and giving.

We need to simplify our jobs if possible, but this is seldom easy.

Therefore, know your important metric and stay focused on it.

Food for Thought

First, stop doing the unnecessary stuff. Trust me—we all do stuff because we think someone else must have it. Ask.

Second, stop doing the smaller stuff (careful, we must do our reporting and detail items). This is often redundant paperwork, the D items—duplicate charts on insignificant metrics. Stop doing redundant tasks and reports. Use the same report for everyone. If corporate leadership or your boss has a standard report, let that be your standard report or ask if you can substitute. This is a huge timesaver: put the report on report writer or a shared drive, then if someone wants to see the data, show him or her how to find it.

Put the report on shared drive. Protect it and let those who are interested go see it. This may save you an e-mail, but those thirty-second tasks add up.

Find a way to do the D items easier. Write a vantage report, link reports, reduce distribution of reports, electronic distribution only of reports, etc.

If you can, delegate, especially the items you don't have time for or hate to do; but someone ultimately has to do all the A items.

Finish something just before you go home every night. This will make you feel like you accomplished something.

Have a things-to-do list. Prioritize it and only work on the top. Put the top priority items on top of the list. Put the bottom three in your "later" drawer.

Have a "later" drawer for stuff to do—if you ever have time.

Try to touch a paper only once and do e-mails only once. Answer them. File them.

Not easy on big jobs but on 90 percent of our work, correspondence is information only. Read it and file it.

We can help each other by reducing distribution lists and reducing "reply all" e-mails.

Treat everyone with respect and hopefully they will treat you with the same respect. Talk about problems using data to take the personalities out of issues.

Swiss cheese on really big jobs—start a little bit at a time and poke holes in it until there is only a little left to finish.

Do the job you hate the most first and get it done. Do the biggest job first and get it done; at least do part of it.

Make it fun! Make it a game. It is more serious than that but let's try to make it fun. Life really is almost a game and the question is how to keep score. Winning the game depends on you. For me it is how many bicycles can I own, Chocolate, Change, and New things to investigate. How many people can I help? How many times a day can I laugh? Grandchildren. How many e-mails can I write (LOL)? Some stress is good and can be fun. Playing cards can be fun, but at $100 a hand? Golf can be fun, but at $100 a hole, it can be major stress. Whitewater rafting can be stressful but it is a rush and tons of fun. Going down a hill on a bicycle at fifty miles an hour is stressful, but fun—if you are an accomplished bicyclist.

In order to win the game at work, we must help our fellow employees, keep our customers happy, make our financial numbers, etc. Every day is a new hand. If this were poker, what card would you play? Think of the statistics and the chances and play your hand accordingly. Tomorrow you will be dealt another hand. You can prepare and learn more about how to play poker but every new deck restarts the statistics. You won't win every hand, but if you win 65 or 70 percent of the hands (i.e. make 65 percent or 70 percent right decisions), you will be a winner.

Make work fun. Think of it as a strategic chess game where you have to plan three or four moves ahead. Think of winning every three or four poker hands. Don't think of it as one bad move means death, darkness, or failure. There will be another game tomorrow.

So, play at work until it is fun!

You Are Your Mirror

I believe that given time our employees begin to act more and more like their boss (scary thought). This is good and bad. They will emulate our good or bad behavior, actions and decisions, especially if we have metrics. Their reviews and increases are based on metrics that we developed and deemed important.

This becomes even more magnified because people tend to hire people like themselves. Here is the danger.

If you and I have some bad habits, our people will tend to develop similar bad habits. If you and I don't pay attention to detail or don't follow rules, policies, and procedures, hours worked, metrics, etc., our employees won't, either.

You may miss great opportunities and solutions because you are thinking alike.

Conclusion:

Try to hire people different than you are.
Be thankful for people who are different than you are, or the rest of your staff, and encourage independent thought and biases.

Make sure you are leading by example. They are watching!

This is partially why it is good to promote some from within and hire some from outside.

Coaches

We are all leaders, coaches, and workers; it just depends on the time, place, and the task to define which hat we are wearing.

I believe we all have individual skills, talents, or gifts. I believe those skills, talents, and gifts do not usually come naturally. They often must be developed. Lance Armstrong, Tiger Woods, and Michael Jordan were not born great athletes. They all worked hard to develop their skills. They may have been born with natural ability, but that alone would not have made them great. I love the story about how Michael Jordan was cut from his early high school basketball team because he was not good enough.

When we are the coach, sometimes we must train and retrain and retrain. Some say three times in three different situations; I personally think it is seven times. The main point is that when we train, we must teach why and how and have patience. When we are the worker, we can only hope we have a coach who is patient.

The measure of a true coach is to know each player's capabilities as follows:

A player may not know he is making a mistake but has the skill to make the play. He just needs to be told "why" it needs to be done.

Sometimes the player may not know how and does not have the ability. It will take a lot of practice and training—the person may need to be more than instructions. He or she may need to know why and how.

Then there is the player who knows how to do it, knows he or she made a mistake, and will fix it next time.

Depending on the day and the incident, a student can have any of the above, and it is the coach's or trainer's task to determine which teaching or training tool to use.

As a coach or trainer you must decide which is the case. Your students' success is dependent on your skill as a coach.

When you are the student, you must recognize the above and ask for help when you don't know. Questions are free.

Right or wrong, when someone fails after I have trained, I always feel that part of his or her failure is part of my failure to coach.

Have a great day! Be a great coach today.

Focus

When I was much, much younger, I enjoyed powerlifting. Powerlifting events were very brief, often less than sixty seconds for a single lift. I was not very good and never won any events, but I enjoyed the competition. I always set goals for lifts depending on my training and would often try to set new personal bests during the actual competition.

When I was in my twenties, lifting was easy; when I was forty-five years old it took a lot of work, practice, preparation, and focus during the actual lift. If I wanted to make my goal target, I had to remove everything from my mind but the single objective. I had to rehearse in my mind the positive outcome.

Strangely, when I was running marathons, it was the same yet almost the opposite. I had to focus or remove my mind from the current pain and focus on something else, somewhere else. In both cases it required tremendous focus. Not being an expert I would guess that baseball, football, golf, and many other sports require extreme mental rehearsal and focus.

Eli Goldratt also has many articles about "Critical Chain" and project management. His whole premise is to focus on the vital three projects. Work on those and only those three until they are complete. If you don't have anything to do on those three projects because of a constraint somewhere else, go stand by the desk of the person who is holding you up.

Goldratt talks about extreme focus and he assumes you know this is your number one priority on your number one constraint. He calls it "multitasking." He suggests we never multitask more than three projects at once and stay focused on those issues that return a known measurable benefit.

Keep your eye on the ball. Know your top three projects and what you expect to get from each. WORK ONLY ON THEM!

FOOD FOR THOUGHT

Who to Blame

Have you ever had something go really wrong and you are really upset?

Your first thought is "Whose fault is this? I want their head" or "I want them to pay me for my loss" or "Why did they do that? They need to apologize" or "That was really stupid, now I have to work Saturday to make up for that mistake" or "I can never trust that person again!" I had that happen to me and I am always very quick to be upset, but I have forced myself to control my immediate anger.

One time when my son was ten and he was mowing the lawn on my Cub Cadet, he was driving really fast. He was driving so fast he was taking corners on two wheels. I yelled at him to slow down. Boy, was I mad. My other son said, "Dad, you never showed him how to stop or slow down!" He was right. It was my error. I had not communicated correctly and I had not trained him properly.

When I stop to think about what part I played in the error, I more often than not realize I could have prevented it, I could have done it myself, or it was my responsibility all along. I am not saying I was directly at fault, but indirectly. Most of the time I did not communicate and did not listen, or I misunderstood. An example is I ask my wife to take my truck to get the oil changed and she forgets. Should I get mad at her because she forgot, or should I get mad at myself for being too lazy to do it after work myself?

So when something goes wrong, be careful who you blame.

Jump in and Paddle

I am sure you have heard the term, "Take up the cross," or "Be a torch-bearer." What do these terms mean?

Sometimes it is difficult to go against the flow; but if it is right, it is right. It is certainly more difficult to swim upstream but sometimes much more fun and much more enlightening.

Often, it is at great risk that we carry the torch. There are not always a lot of maps for direction and sometimes no one has gone there before. That is the fun part—going where no one else has dared to go.

Listening to the story is not the same as reading the book. Reading the book is not the same as being part of the adventure. Watching the television show *Survivor* is not the same as actually being part of the group. You may get a feel for what is happening but the real adventure is to participate.

It is wonderful to admire the adventurer. It is another to follow and yet another to be part of the exploration team! It can be fun and adventurous, so this is your call to action. Just because you have never tried the idea and/or it was not your idea does not make it wrong.

Help your fellow employees learn new skills and try new ideas. Look at every idea as "What is good about it?"

You have to love change. It is a great adventure!

IF YOUR NEW IDEA COULD MAKE THE CUSTOMER HAPPIER, EMPLOYEES HAPPIER, AND IMPROVE THE FINANCIALS AND IT IS EASY TO CHANGE BACK IF IT FAILS, TRY IT.

People Skills

I realized, as I kept editing this book and rewriting and re-editing, that this was going take me a lifetime to get right. So I have decided to publish my ideas hoping that some small part will help you in the continuous communications process. I want to thank Stef, my son, Rob, and my wife for their contribution to this volume. Obviously I needed some direction and input.

We all need a touch of humility, a smidgeon of self-confidence, a ton of listening skills, empathy, and a dash of compassion!

There are a lot of people who should be writing this "food for thought" epistle about people skills other than me. Since communications and people skills are so instrumental in improvement, we have a need for such a discussion. It does not hurt for me to remind myself so that I might continue to improve. I will attempt to discuss how we can all improve our people skills.

Last night Karen (my wife) and I were discussing people skills. I asked, "What were my people skills like when I was twenty-five or thirty?"

Sorry, she didn't remember (thank goodness). But we both remembered that I laughed a lot and liked people. I am sure I was a typical young engineer who had very little empathy, but as I grew older I had several bosses who were great people-people. I tried to observe and copy their people skills.

Ray Hartenstine in Philadelphia was without question always perfectly honest and open with everyone, but very caring and tactful. Bob Ruffin at Bendix (Allied Signal) was a great listener and very empathetic. He could communicate with anyone at any level and seemed to really know everyone's personal interests. There was Jim Fox at Bendix who was my hero at tough love. He coined the phrase TROOP (Total Respect Of Other People) and he lived it. He treated everyone fairly but set tough, high standards. He did not appear to have favorites but was compassionate.

I believe you can develop your people skills if you have a true, sincere desire and if you like people.

Stef and I discussed how to improve people skills and the way of life at GE. He stated, and I agree, that often it is not what you read, seminars you attend, or observing your mentor. Most often it is a significant event in your life. The loss of a parent or friend, taking care of a grandparent with Alzheimer's or a handicapped child, losing your job or your business due to people issues are all significant events that will help us change our value system and thus our people skills.

So you say you don't want to waste time and energy improving your people skills. My response is that you will be far more successful, your projects far more timely, and your job a lot more fun and rewarding working *with* people rather than against them. It takes only minutes a day to improve your people skills, so the obstacle is all in your mind. What have you got to lose? If you try, your people skills can't get worse. ☺

Food for Thought

Gifts and Giving, Giving your Talents

There are many stories about giving. We see it all around us, especially immediately after September 11, 2001.

I want to talk about three things relative to giving, yet they are all very similar:

- Compounding
- Gifts that keep on giving
- Building

Compounding. We all have talents we are born with and then develop—mathematical, verbal, musical, detailed or organizational, physical, logical, etc. We all have some learned skills—car mechanics, computer programming, etc. We all have some areas of expertise from personal experiences.

If we teach others some skills using our talents from some of the skills we have developed and wisdom from our experiences, we have compounded the speed with which both of us can improve.

If we teach others to fish, together we can feed more people.

If we teach each other the principles of Smed (Quick Change), we can get more ideas on how to make changeover faster.

Sharing your talent with many people compounds the benefit and the rate of improvement.

When others share back their talents, the improvement compounds even more rapidly.

Gifts. Some gifts are: "If you give a person a fish, they'll fish for a day. But if you train a person to fish, they'll fish for a lifetime" (quote by Dan Quale). This is similar to compounding, yet different. Some gifts have ways of coming back. For example, I can buy a candy bar and enjoy it for five minutes or I can give it to a five-year-old child who has never had a candy bar and watch him or her eat it and enjoy the memory for a lifetime.

Some gifts keep on giving to ourselves. Sharing gifts, talents, and experiences with others in such a way that it helps them improve their lives has a way of giving back to ourselves.

When we give, we are not just giving a candy bar; we are building lives and futures.

Sometimes we look too short-term at the prospect of giving and, of course, sometimes it is all perspective.

We can look at Thermal Forming as molding a piece of plastic or as making a medical delivery system or as making an orthopedic device that will help someone walk again.

I love the story about three stonemasons. When asked what they were doing, the first said that he was chipping stone, the second said, "I am building a cathedral," and the third said, "I am teaching these three apprentices to build other cathedrals."

I hope you do build cathedrals, but our real objective is to teach our fellow employees how to build cathedrals.

CHAPTER 8

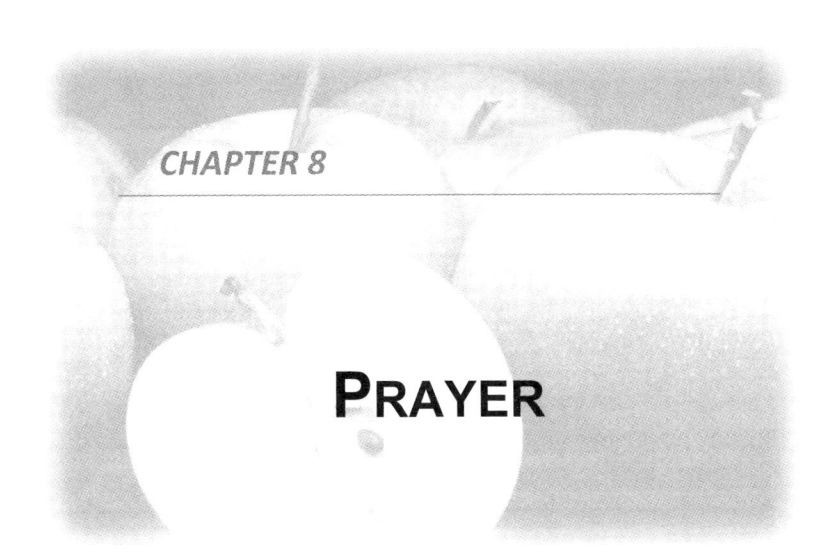

PRAYER

For years I thought I prayed a lot but I now realize that I didn't. I always thought you needed to be in a quiet place, alone and where you could close your eyes, kneel, and commune with God. However, a while back, one of our pastors gave a sermon about prayer and how God is listening no matter the time of day or the place.

From that time on I tried to pray often. I would pray at a traffic light, waiting for a train at a railroad crossing, while jogging or walking, driving to work, during television commercials, etc. All I needed to do was say, "God, please help Dave, Marjory, Judy, Randy's family, etc." I have a list of those I lift in prayer often. I try to do it daily. When asked to commit to five minutes in prayer a day, I thought that it would be a piece of cake. It has been, if you consider all the time that I use to pray.

I also have bad days when I pray asking God to help me cope. Sometimes it is as simple as saying, "God, please help me. Please lift this burden. I will do as You lead." Sometimes my personal prayers are just thanking God for all the gifts He has given me, or for the beautiful day.

Years ago, when a friend was ill or had a family issue, I would tell him or her, "We are thinking about you!" I think it was my son

Food for Thought

who suggested I change just one word to, "We are *praying* for you." At first I found this difficult, but the more I said it, the easier it became. I am still working on just saying, "Let's pray about it together now." I am praying for the emotional strength and maturity to enable me say that.

It is wonderful if you have time to set aside for structured and uninterrupted prayer. If you use my rules, you can't say that you can't find time.

Let's pray about it!

"God, give us the maturity, conviction, and emotional strength to pray daily. Amen"

So, if you see someone driving down Rt. 15 with his or her eyes closed, you will know who it is. (LOL)

Pride

As I was going to sleep last night, I thought of a great quote on the negatives of pride. I thought to myself, as I was half asleep, "Wow, this is a quote worth remembering like 'We have not yet begun to fight' by Nathan Hale." This morning I had forgotten the quote and only remembered it was something about pride.

We want our employees to be proud of their work, of each other, our company, and our products; but we never want to be so proud that we overlook a new or better idea. Failure to see or accept a better idea has been the failure of thousands of managers and companies.

It is okay to be proud of people. It is dangerous to be blind with pride and overlook new designs, new processes, or policies and procedures. It is often the companies' own rules that cause their demise.

It is okay to be so proud that you think you are the greatest and say like Ali, "Float like a butterfly and sting like a bee," but there will be a day soon that you are no longer the greatest. We must constantly look for ways to change and improve.

Have you seen the film *The Paradigm?* The Swiss invented the digital watch, yet never patented it. Their paradigm was that watches are mechanical and they missed the whole shift in the market.

Be proud but be willing to look at every idea as an opportunity to improve. Your biases can be your failure. The best process today may be the second best tomorrow.

We must strive for continual improvement.

Trust

To be better at any task, we need some basic tools:

Have a foundation in the skill and understand the fundamentals (i.e., tool geometry, feeds and speeds, materials, tolerances, gages, etc. for a machinist). Training, training, training. Learning, learning, learning.

Keep learning, moving, and growing in knowledge and tools (i.e., 5S, professional societies, read professional magazines and books, benchmark our competitors, trade shows). Ongoing training, ongoing learning.

Know the big picture. It is okay to work on details as long as it supports the big picture. Every local decision must support the global goals of the organization. Share the data.

Communicate and share your knowledge. Help others grow and see the big picture. Share the data.

We must practice what we preach, walk the talk, etc. We must be predictable and consistent. We must be obsessive about 5S.

We need to be happy with what we are doing, happy with who we are, proud of what we do. But, we must continuously try to improve everything we do. We all have special skills. We all contribute. Everyone's uniqueness is needed but we must all work to improve.

Invest in others. Share data and knowledge and they in turn will share with you. Eli Goldratt says we are only as strong as our weakest link. We are only as good as our weakest, least trained employee. As that person improves, we improve as a team.

Trust each other. Be honest with each other. Expect that you are being treated fairly and treat others fairly. Assume the best from others.

Things are Seldom as We Perceive

It is a beautiful day! Our expectations or the Pygmalion effect often colors our perception. We can usually meet our self-expectations.

I am reminded of maybe fifteen years ago when a young engineer came into my office in a terrible mood. His four-year-old had just spilled a bucket of paint his wife was using all over their new carpet in their new house. My reply was to tell him to calm down because it could have been much worse. He could not understand. I stated that it could have been a pan of boiling water off the stove that his four-year-old spilled on herself. He paused and left my office. I overheard him call his wife and say he would see her that evening and that they would go look for some new carpet. Sometimes things are not as we first perceive!

I have been trying to pass the Indiana vehicle and motorcycle driver's license test. I passed the car/truck test on the second try with a 100 percent grade, but have not taken the motorcycle test a second time. I have now read the motorcycle license book four times. In that book a comment is made on how a vehicle accident is seldom a random act. It is often avoidable by both people (i.e., with all the people running red lights, it is best to look both ways when your light is green).

Safety and quality issues are often the result of multiple errors and the errors are seldom visible at first review. Almost always several people had the opportunity to prevent the issue.

Take my young engineering friend, for example. His wife should have had a heavy drop cloth or should have had someone watching the four-year-old. It was not an accident—it could have been prevented.

FOOD FOR THOUGHT

If we work just a little smarter, look both ways, check an extra part to print, mop up that slippery floor, and pick up that bolt on the floor, we can prevent an accident or quality issue.

So. We can learn from each other and we should never judge a book by its cover. We should try to benchmark others in our industry and learn from others through reading, industry shows, and professional societies, etc. We need to share our best practices with each other.

Hello, I am a Christian

Don't focus on faults, focus on encouragement. Don't focus on faults, be thankful for the good traits you have.

Just a few weeks after we moved to Warsaw, we started attending the First United Methodist Church. A few weeks after that I joined the church choir. I did not want to miss singing all the wonderful Christmas music.

Choir practice is every Wednesday night at 7 PM. On my first practice, the choir met in the sanctuary, on my second practice no one was in the sanctuary, so I headed to the choir room. Being me, I was early. I walked into the choir room and none of the faces were familiar but I did not know many, so nothing seemed out of place. The choir folders were all missing and I looked and felt a little bewildered.

A friendly face came up to me and said, "Can I help you?" I stated I was looking for my choir folder and choir practice. They stated, "Oh, this is AA, choir meets in the sanctuary."

Well, I probably belonged in AA twenty-five years ago but now I was just looking for a box to hide in. After thinking about this for a while, I decided it was funny but also providence. I have a new call line. "Hello, my name is Alec McPherson and I am a Christian." For years I was afraid to admit it. The second step is to be willing to say to people, "I will pray for you."

Be Profound

First thought

Easy decisions are easy by definition. Profound! But, when a decision makes more work for you—I mean a *lot* of extra work—or if a decision creates pain, it is a hard decision. Those tough decisions will really test your values.

When I was younger I used to think my efforts were good enough but now I say to myself, "It will only take a few extra seconds to wipe off that wrench and put it away instead of leaving it greasy on my bench." At the end of the day I will never miss those extra seconds. In fact, at the end of the week it may save me time when I am looking for that clean wrench.

Second thought

Be Prepared. Profound! This somewhat follows the first thought. You will be better prepared if you have put that tool away (i.e., a place for everything, and everything in its place)! But being prepared is more than putting away your tools. It is being prepared for change, looking for change, assisting others in accepting change, being willing to accept that someone else has a better idea, being willing to accept that my idea did not work and changing back, being prepared to share information and skills with others, being prepared not to blame someone but to look for why!

Third thought

Be an Optimist. Profound! Negativism is depressing and contagious. It is time-consuming. I must admit that I have bad days, but thankfully I have more good days than bad days. Sometimes when in a dark mood, I need a friend to pull me out. It is okay to be a cautious optimist, but look for ways to improve. Know that there is a better way.

Fourth thought
Geese are always self-managed teams when flying in formation.

They rotate leadership. One pulls until tired and then they rotate. They fly in a V so that the others on their wing can fly easier, using their updraft to experience less turbulence. If one goose is injured, another goose stays with it. A flock of geese are a real team.

We can certainly be smarter and better to our fellow workers than the geese.

Empathy

I only know what I see on the Internet and on the news. I have had to fire a lot of people throughout my career, even some personal friends. Sometimes it was for performance and sometimes it was just because business was poor. The last time was just two months ago when I released my director of quality. Every time I say "this is the last time I will fire someone." It is never easy and often personally painful. The especially painful ones were the ones I had personally hired and then, when they did not perform, I had to give them a severance package.

I still feel that I am partially to blame for their failure. I tried to help them after it was evident that they were not performing but eventually it was evident that they were not going to get the job done. However, in every case, I have tried to give them a good severance package along with outplacement service and in almost every case they ended up better off. They knew they were not performing and deep down were unhappy with their own job. You have my empathy. Bobby or Joe or Ann will be better off in his or her next position whatever that may be. But, it is still a tough decision.

Rules that we Teach

"Wisdom is avoiding all thoughts that weaken you"—Dr. Wayne Dyer.

I don't know if I totally agree, but it is a quote that I heard recently, and it is thought-provoking. My translation of the quote might be, "What you think about controls your attitude." It makes me think that we are often in control of our own destiny if we can focus our thoughts and attitudes. However, sometimes we need a little coaching.

Sometimes, as we are being coached, we make errors and need forgiveness. Okay, let me try to state where I am going. We are all teachers, coaches, and students at different times and on different subjects. We can help each other and thus the gain of the whole by sharing and teaching, coaching, mentoring, etc. As a teacher or coach it is our responsibility to teach the process.

When an error is made it is the teacher's responsibility to understand the root cause of the error and not to blame the student but to understand why the error was made. Sometimes the error is lack of understanding of the process or goal, sometimes it is the lack of skill, and sometimes it is a matter of lack of priority. The teacher needs to know and understand which is the root cause. Knowing the root cause of why the error was made is much more important than knowing who made the error because it allows us to teach the process better.

In summary, don't be overwhelmed by errors that we have made. Instead, understand why we made the errors and make adjustments in the process. Share your gained knowledge and focus on tomorrow.

Food for Thought

CHAPTER 9

BE PROUD

I have told many people that this is the best company that I have ever worked for. Of course, I live in my own little dream world. It is the best company for a lot of reasons, including great people to work with, a great product that helps people, a growing and dynamic company, and we make a profit. I do believe we should tell others where we work and why we are proud of where we work. Of course, I am assuming that you like to work here. I would like to think we work hard to make our company a great place to work. We can't just say it—we must believe it. We can't just believe it—we must live it. Be proud of what you do and where you work.

We must all work at making our company a better place to work. A great place to work is not good enough unless everyone agrees. We can't just be proud, we must make it so!

So, I was thinking. What does it take for us to be proud of where we work? I think the following:

1. TROOP—Total Respect Of Other People (coined by Jim Fox). We need to respect our fellow employees.
2. People, Customer, Products, and Community. If a company takes care of these four issues, employees are usually proud of their place of employment. Opportunities, job enrichment, involvement, flexible,

fairness, clean and safe, fair pay, share in financial rewards with goal sharing, community service, a product that helps people live better lives, customer focus on quality and delivery, and customer value. I think these are most of the basics that give us a warm feeling of pride in our jobs.

Talk about it. Wear your company T-shirt and cap with pride. A company has to earn the pride, but the pride comes from the employees.

Big Picture

Remember the big picture! Customer! EBITDA! People!

When everything seems to be going wrong! Scrap, late deliveries, customers want expedites, new employees need training, etc.

Remember to look up and look at the big picture.

We aren't just running machines, welding parts, assembling parts, polishing parts, inspecting and packing parts. We are not just making surgical instruments. We are changing people's lives for the better.

I remember my wife's grandfather in the early 1970s using crutches and being almost wheelchair bound due to his bad knees. He was a young sixty-nine-year-old. Today, it might be different for him. I remember my Grandmother McPherson falling and breaking her hip in 1963. They could not repair it; she was a bed patient for the rest of her life.

Wow, the changes we have made in people's lives. You are not just a bricklayer or mason, you are a building a library. You are not just a CNC machinist, you are assisting a doctor.

Sometimes we have to STOP and think about what we are doing and how important it is to others. What you are doing is more important than the products we ship and more than the profit (though that is important) because the value in your daily work affects the quality of life of someone.

Enjoy. Look up and remember you are helping someone.

Do You Remember Your First Real Job?

I don't mean those part-time jobs we had in high school or college; I had several of those. I was a pizza cook, a gas station attendant, a tire mechanic at Sears, a janitor in a women's department store and later at a hospital, an Amway soap-mixer, forklift driver, welder, paint line operator, press operator, etc. Do you want more? (LOL) I am talking about your first forty-hour-a-week job that you expected was to be your career.

My first full-time job was at Chevrolet Flint Engine. I was really excited, full of wonder and high expectations. It was a wonderful training program for eight months. I worked as an hourly person in maintenance, engineering, safety, quality, accounting, and production. I spent one to four weeks in every department. Then at the old age of twenty-three I was a production supervisor on the final engine assembly line with fifty-four employees. Wow! What an experience.

What I remember most about my first full-time job were the people who worked around me and my training supervisors' first eight months. What great people. I knew absolutely nothing and they helped me get started. Some of those training supervisors treated me like a human being and actually gave me meaningful work hoping I could contribute during my weeklong or two-week stay. Others asked me to sit quietly in a chair and observe. I don't need to tell you which I preferred. Sitting in a chair for a week was extremely boring.

Those people training me had nothing to gain by helping me, but so many gave me their time and words of wisdom.

I think we have the same opportunity with our new employees. How will they remember us ten or twenty years from now?

We need to treat all our new employees with respect and a healthy helping hand. They can then become full contributing members quicker. They will be happier employees and ten to twenty years from now they will be the old timers welcoming the new people.

No Man is an Island

"No man is an island, entire of itself; every man is a piece of the continent, a part of the main. If a clod be washed away by the sea, Europe is the less, as well as if a promontory were, as well as if a manor of thy friends' or of thine own were. Any man's death diminishes me, because I am involved in mankind. And therefore never send to know for whom the bell tolls; it tolls for thee . . . " John Donne (1572–1631).

One person—one man—can't win a football game by himself. A great individual effort can certainly make a difference but even Barry Sanders or Walter Payton could not win ball games by themselves. Without a great offensive line they were nothing, even with great offensive lines but without a great defense, they were on mediocre teams. However, one man can lose a game. One poor performance can cost the team dearly through a fumble or a dropped pass or a missed play.

It is the same in business. No one person can make our company successful without everyone working together—like a highly tuned racing engine. We must be exceptional in our execution of the fundamentals and we must always stay focused on the "customer" and on "making money now and in the future." If we improve "customer delight" through zero defects, zero errors, and keeping our promises, we will take giant steps to delighting our customers.

You are important! We need great individual efforts, but it's even more important that we help each other improve first-piece inspections, training, etc. Learn from our mistakes; teach others so they avoid repeating those mistakes

Clean it up for us

A very good friend of mine, who has since passed away, had a great housekeeping program called "Clean it Up for Us." Tom Schulstrom had a wonderful idea that worked exceptionally well. Tom was the Plant Manager for the large and very dirty Bendix Foundry. He declared, "Why should we clean up our own house and yard for visitors? We are the ones who are here all day every day. Let's clean it up for us." The employees did and it was the cleanest foundry I ever saw. I have toured sixteen foundries that I remember and the Bendix foundry in St. Joseph was the cleanest by far.

The same applies to many areas. Be proud of ourselves. Have a great attitude for ourselves. We must be proud of the things we do, clean our plant for ourselves, and have high quality and on-time delivery for ourselves. Have confidence that we can be the best. I am not suggesting we be overconfident or arrogant. Just be proud of the things we do well. We can learn how to do things better and while we are learning, think positive thoughts. If we are proud of what we do and we work to stay the best by benchmarking the best, the rest will come.

Dr. Norman Vincent Peale had a message he gave every New Years that went something like the following:

We become what our attitudes are. If your attitude is that tomorrow is going to be a bad day, it's a bad day before it starts. You have condemned it to be a bad day and so it will be a bad day. If, on the other hand, you affirm that tomorrow is going to be a wonderful day, it's a wonderful day before you ever begin because you have affirmed it is a wonderful day. . . .

The above words are his, not mine. But, I wholly agree. The Pygmalion effect—the positive expectation of favorable results, wins.

When I took a Dale Carnegie course in 1971, they had us put a note on our bathroom mirror. It was to say, "Today will be a wonderful day." But I wrote on my note, "Today will be a great adventure!" They even had us carry a one-inch square mirror in our pocket that we were to look at when we had negative thoughts. We were to look into the mirror and state to ourselves, "Today is a great day!"

I recognize that not everything in this world is peachy or rosy but we can always look for the good and the positive. Sometimes it is hard to find, but it is there. I recognize that I am oversimplifying, but we can make it a better day just by expecting the best.

Remember the story of the poor family with small twin boys? One was a pessimist and the other the eternal optimist. On Christmas one year the boys awoke to a large pile of horse manure in their front yard. The pessimist said that pile really stinks and turned away. The optimist dove in and was screaming with joy, "With all this horse manure, there must be a pony in here someplace!"

So, we must be happy with ourselves for ourselves. Be proud of what we do for ourselves. The rest will come.

Have a great adventure today!

Walk to Emmaus

I am always asking questions, often of myself. SOMETIMES I ANSWER. Frequently I do not have an immediate answer.

Below are some examples of questions I ask of myself. You may ask them of yourself.

1. Will I recognize opportunities for improvement when they present themselves? Or will my own biases and my own paradigms blind me from seeing the idea? Will I be so defensive when someone else has an idea that I fail to recognize its significance? And, of course, if I recognize the significance, will I take action? I wish I would just look for the good in it when someone else has an idea different than mine.
2. Will I properly reward new ideas whether good or bad? Will I reward the process of improvement as well as the actual accomplishment?
3. Will we all work together as a team and focus on team goals, setting aside individual goals with the expectation that individual goals will be met if the team goals are met?
4. Will we strive for and believe together that we can continuously improve?
5. How can I improve so that I can communicate and lead better?
6. How can we train our employees so we all work smarter and have fun together?
7. Are we "sharing the bread and fishes"? Do we have the proper reward and recognition systems in place?
8. How will we identify the vital few "TTD" (action items)? Do we know what impact they will have? Are we staying focused on the vital few? Have we communicated these vital few to our people?

You know me, just asking questions! But I ask them of myself also.

TROOP

1. You must respect other people, Total Respect of Other People (Jim Fox).
2. I like the golden rule, "Do unto others . . ." and "never ask someone to do something that you are not willing to do."
3. You must address differences by defining the problem and agreeing on the problem. Yes, there are differences in biases, but more often the difference is the perception of the real problem. Then together analyze the data and discuss solutions.
4. My son, Rev. Rob, adds, "Often our frustration has nothing to do with the perceived problem at all. Often the real problem is our feelings about the other person and we have created an emotional barrier to hearing them."
5. Spend more time listening. Really try to see things from the other person's perspective. Communicate your position clearly but allow others to disagree with you. Rev. Rob adds, "Don't try to force others to see things the way you do. Make it a point to stay in contact and relationship with those who disagree with you."
6. Assume all people are honest until proven several times they are not. Several times, make sure; often perceived dishonesty is miscommunications.
7. Read Stephen Covey's book, *The 7 Habits of Highly Effective People.* Covey adds that these books are also great, *The One Minute Manger* series by Spencer Johnson and Kenneth Blanchard or *What They Don't Teach You at Harvard Business School* by Mark McCormack. I particularly like Stephen Covey's bank concept.
8. Get to know someone else's personal interests. Remember Will Rogers who said, "I never met a man I did not like." He went on to say that once he met a person and he got to know that person, he would find some common interest and some common sense of good.
9. Identify the person or persons you are having the most communications problems with and try to find out why.

Try to find out one thing you have in common. Try to discuss that one thing several times a week for one or two minutes.
10. Be sincere.
11. Don't have favorites. Treat all people fairly and consistently. You can be tough and demanding but you must be tough and demanding with everyone.
12. Use a touch of humility, a smidgeon of self-confidence, a ton of listening skills, empathy. and a dash of compassion!
13. IN SUMMARY, PEOPLE SKILLS ARE OFTEN COMMUNICATIONS SKILLS ALONG WITH CONSISTENCY AND CARING!

Food for Thought

CHAPTER 10

GOALS FOR THE NEW YEAR, FOOD FOR THOUGHT 101

Have I told you that I do this annual goals thing? It drives my wife crazy and I have been writing annual goals for more than twenty years. I call them goals. Some might call them resolutions. I try to have at least one goal in each of the following areas: work, mental, physical, spiritual, financial, family, social, and something new. I did not accomplish all my goals last year. I seldom have. I accomplished approximately 75 percent of them.

An example of a mental goal might be reading 6 books during the year. Physical might be bicycling 3,500 miles, bench 225 pounds, or walk/run 500 miles.

This year I thought I needed a "theme" to tie all the goals together. My new theme is to listen more, talk less, be more patient, eat less, exercise more, give less stress, receive less stress, and celebrate life more. Notice that none of my goals are to send fewer e-mails, though that might be a good goal.

We all could use a little more fun and a little less stress. Some stress is good but too much stress and uncontrolled stress is bad for your body and mind. What is stress? What causes Stress?

- Change or something different
- Unplanned bad results

- Lack of data or lack of information
- Confrontation and disagreement
- Surprises
- Seemingly unreasonable demands by internal and external customers
- Too much work for the time allowed or working too many hours
- Not listening, not agreeing on a problem statement prior to working on a solution

Yes, I do mean that sometimes we have stress at work!

I didn't even mention personal stress such as money, family, teenagers, aging parents or grandparents, health, and competition with brother or neighbor.

What can we do to minimize stress? Food can cause stress if your diet is poor (e.g., too much sugar). Watch what you eat. Eat less sugar.

Some stress is good. It is when it is unmanaged that it is bad. Stress can cause us to think smarter and come up with new innovative ideas. Too much stress causes us to spin our wheels.

We can manage stress by talking to each other using facts, not assumptions and conjecture. Talk to each other and make sure you have both correctly identified the problem statement. If we can agree on the problem statement (which is tough) we can work on solutions together. If we can't agree on the problem statement, we are both wasting our time talking about solutions.

Stress starts to reduce with trust. No trust leads to high stress. High levels of trust make stress manageable.

So, for the next New Year, we all need to have one of our goals be to listen more, talk less. If we want to start the New Year on the right foot, we need to establish goals and we need a plan to achieve them. We also need to identify how we will measure success.

Last year was a great year; this year can be even better for you personally.

P.S. Never assume you understand the intent of a message. Ask! More stress is caused by misunderstanding and assumption than is caused by fact.

Blue Sky

Provoking thought: seldom does one person have all the answers and it is often a lot easier to ask questions. Sometimes we can anticipate the questions. We all need to do a little "Blue Sky thinking" on our own or in our small work teams about ways to improve more quickly. Sometimes it takes data along with that creativity to head in the correct direction.

My task is to measure, teach, motivate, communicate, and inspire (provoke thought) ideas and action. Invite participation and new ideas to excite and stir people toward continual improvement in their work processes.

It is almost like rowing or sculling. In scull teams of six or more, I believe they have a coxswain, or captain, calling out the beat. He or she is watching the team and the competition and inspiring (provoking) the team to keep the beat and pull evenly. Hopefully everyone on the team stays in the boat with both oars in the water stroking in harmony with the rest of the team and all oars pulling equally, keeping the boat traveling in a straight line. The coxswain's job is to know the team players and to sense their energy. The coxswain's job is just as important during training. Train hard. Race hard!

We are a fleet of rowing teams. We have several business units all working individually and yet together. Each business unit has a captain who is calling out the beat. We also are competing in the Olympics but we only win if all of our boats finish in the top five.

I am not an expert at rowing or an expert machinist but I hope I can measure, teach, and inspire you to work as a team. We can all teach, reward, recognize, encourage, incite, provoke, and use data, data, data to win in business. We need to row smarter, row harder, strengthen the weakest team member, and pull together.

When closing an old year and starting a new year, we are often reminded that competition is fierce. We must deliver 100 percent quality and 100 percent on time. In order to do this we must improve slightly every day. Look for new ways to improve.

Have a great day and think customer!

We are Healers

We aren't just machinists. We aren't just designers of instruments. We are healers.

The quality and flexibility of our products give the physician a better opportunity to heal. We work to make a living. We work smarter and harder for job satisfaction and job security and so that our company can make a profit. But greater than this, we are helping others enjoy a better quality of life as a result of our products.

My personal charter or mantra is as follows, "To give a little more each day than I receive." Othy gives us all that opportunity. If we share knowledge, have a great attitude, and trust of our fellow workers, we can have a lot of fun together.

I come from a very close family. I remember once a long time ago telling one of my sisters that it looked like she was gaining a little weight. Wow, was she upset; I must have hit a tender spot. Anyway, by the end of the evening, she still liked me. I have never told her that again. My point is that even though it was dumb on my part to mention her weight, she forgave me. She still liked me and trusted me.

Sometimes all of us do and say things that we later regret. That should not diminish all the good things we try to do. There is always a difference between intentionally offending someone and meaning well. Sometimes what we mean and what we attempt doesn't quite come out right.

Give our friends and fellow workers a little room for error and assume the best. We mean well!

We need to get past those miscommunications and believe that we are all here trying to do a good job for each other and for the company. We must realize that all of us make errors. We hope they are few.

We tend to give our close friends the benefit of the doubt, as we should.

10 best days of your life

Take a minute think about the ten best days of your life. Why were they so memorable?

Think about three people who had the greatest positive influence on your life and why. You should write these three or better yet, call them and tell them how thankful you are.

You may also take another minute and think about your five worst days.

I had a hard time coming up with just ten best days and I would like to think I still have a few of my ten best days left. In every case, my best days were the result of giving or receiving gifts from people as opposed to giving to myself. Yes, my first date with my wife and the birth of our three children make the list. But other best days involve work and friends!

I could not limit my most influential people to three. There were my parents, two high school teachers, a pastor in my youth, an engineering mentor, and a boss mentor among the group of people who had a significant impact on my life.

At the time, a few of my worst days were work-related but now, years later, they weren't really so bad. In fact, as I look back, some of them ended up being a significant positive influence on my life.

What will we remember ten years from now? Will some of these days or these people we work with be our best days or our most influential people? We can't make influential people or most memorable days for ourselves, but we can for others. Make a difference! Help someone else. Be a mentor. Be a trainer. Be a positive influence. Share your skill and share your knowledge.

Visionary

My wife, Karen, and I were talking about our parents a few days ago. I stated to her that my father had strong opinions. After my older brother left for college, my father and I would spend several hours every night and morning milking cows and picking or sorting apples, and other chores. We frequently talked about current events, history, church, farming, 4-H. There was much discussion around the dinner table with my five sisters and two brothers.

One time, while I was milking cows and not paying a lot of attention, Dad was discussing some of his conservative political issues. He said that I was visionary. I did not pay much attention to the comment at that time. He also had some nicknames for me but we won't go into that.

Sometime, a year or so later when I was a senior, he called me a visionary again. Like a nut I ask my dad what he meant by "visionary." He smiled and said, "You're a daydreamer." I should have left well enough alone, but he was right. I can daydream in the best of meetings, while driving a tractor, milking cows, hunting, fishing, running, biking, etc. I'll bet you can also.

Yes, I frequently dream about "what if." What if I had worked a little harder and won that big match. What if my team had won the big game and had gone on to win the Olympic gold or the

NCAA title? Sometimes I dream about being in college again to get that second chance.

Then when I come to my senses, I realize that every decision I made in my life changed the final outcome. So if I went back and if I had won that title match, if I had won that race, would it have changed my life? The resultant change could be dramatic. Life could have turned out far worse. I might not have gone to Michigan State, not married Karen, become an engineer, had our three wonderful children, or had our even more wonderful grandchildren, or run a Boston Marathon. Maybe I would have never come to know you.

There are so many things in my life that I would not want to change and I would not want to risk. Now, I find it hard to dream about being young again and being given a second chance. I feel very blessed with the experiences I have had in my life. There are a few things I would like to change but not at the risk of changing others.

One of those things I would not want to change is having had the opportunity to have lived in Londonderry, been a member of Londonderry UMC choir, a member of Derry Village Rotary, riding our bicycles three or four times a week around Lake Masabesic, working out on the floor with each of you, MBF sheets, teaching those Smed, Cell, and 5S classes and, of course, having worked with all of you at Symmetry.

The last few years I try to dream about the future. I dream of how I do great things to help other people, how I learn the discipline to practice my piano and become accomplished, how I become ten pounds lighter and bench press 225 pounds, how the plant is so clean that all the employees and all the visitors are in awe, and that our customers are so delighted that we win their best supplier award.

So my challenge to you is to dream about the future of yourselves and our company. Dream to have more fun tomorrow! The best dream is when you help someone else have more fun or to teach someone else a new skill that makes his or her life better and at the same time you learn and you personally change.

In conclusion, and the takeaway from this "Food for thought," is best described by Leo Tolstoy, "Everybody thinks of changing humanity and nobody thinks of changing himself." And by Bill Flanagan's quote to me, "Man cannot change the direction of the wind but he can adjust the sails." I have learned a lot while at Manchester; I have changed more than you will ever know. I hope you have changed and that you will continue to strive to improve personally. It will be a great adventure!

Power of Prayer

When there are so many issues in the world, it seems small to ask for prayer. Let me tell you my story and how sometimes our own prayers just don't seem to be enough. Probably nothing but prayers will make it easier. I know a few of you have been in the same position and prayer works.

Karen and I went to Mayo March 18 for our annual physicals. My company paid for mine and with all of Karen's troubles, we paid for hers. I wanted to make sure she was healthy, especially after all the problems she had had the last several years.

Well, as it turned out she is as healthy as a young racehorse with a resting pulse of 39, blood pressure of 120 over 75, etc. Her mammogram, blood work, chest x-ray, hearing, and everything else was perfect. With a cholesterol count of 175 and HDL of 62 she is going to live for another fifty plus years.

However, I had some unnerving news when I was at Mayo. From the blood work, physical exam, pulse, etc. I was told that I was in remarkable shape. My cholesterol count was 180, HDL 45, blood pressure 120 over 80, and pulse was 55. I had gone there expecting to be told I was in perfect health except for my back. I was right about the back. I have some degeneration of a few discs and a slightly ruptured disc but no real nerve damage and it is fine except that I should never run.

Then, after the EKG and chest x-ray I was told there were a few abnormalities and I needed a few more tests. I have been told this about my EKGs for a long time. I have been told for fifteen years that runners have a different EKG. My EKG is normal on the stress test but is abnormal at rest. So they want me to have an echo EKG or an EBKG (whatever those are). I am not too worried about this. Now the concerned part! I was told I have some clouding or scar tissue on my left lung and they want to do a CT scan. They say it is probably nothing but they needed to confirm that diagnosis! They told me to go to my family physician for further tests. Of course, I did not have a family physician in New Hampshire yet, as I had only recently moved there. Well, it takes forever to get in to see a doctor to have these additional tests and if you know me, you know my type A personality is driving me crazy.

Well, I finally got to see a new family physician. I took her copies of my prior EKGs, and she agreed with me that my heart was fine. The EKGs are identical to the ones I had ten years and fifteen years ago. She even stated that I was on the treadmill twice as long as the average male my age.

She looked at my x-ray results and suggested another x-ray, which we did. Her comment was that I probably had had a fungus or pneumonia sometime in the recent past. Her experience was that this is common in Michigan where I had previously lived. I had the second x-ray and waited for the results.

Well the x-ray results finally came in and guess what? They are normal.

"So, I had prayed, worried, prayed some more, asked God to take my burdens and help me "accept thy will." I guess it worked. I am remarkably healthy, so they say.

Good Guys and Bad Guys

There is the parable about the Pharisees and the Tax Collectors. You know—the good guys and bad guys. The only question was who were the good guys? All businesses have good guys and bad guys. My interpretation of the parable goes, "Don't be deceived into thinking who is the good guy and who is the bad guy." The good guys are not always the guys wearing suits, wearing white hats, and saying yes. The good guys aren't always the people who do everything by all the rules and follow all the procedures.

To me the good guy is the one who realizes we need to change to improve. The good people measure so they know how they are doing. The good guys are the people who recognize their mistakes and make a valiant effort to improve. The good guy recognizes when he has made a mistake, finds out why the mistake was made, and corrects the root cause. The good guy is the one who isn't doing it for show, but knows the real measure of success and contributes for the good of the whole. The good guys aren't perfect. They just want to be. The good guys know who the customer is and always consider the impact on the customer. The real good guys know the score and measure the performance. What is really strange is that we are often a mix of good guy/bad guy. What is good in one situation is bad in another. One is good for today but is bad for tomorrow.

Our goals are to improve customer satisfaction, employee satisfaction, and financial performance. Go forth if you have a decision that improves all three and make that change, especially if the change is easy to reverse. Make those decisions that err on the side of improving on-time delivery and shortening customer lead times.

Results count!

Results vary just due to statistics, so they are not always exactly predictable. Forecasting is the science of knowing that there is variation and expecting variation but looking for a general trend.

Results are not an accident. Results are an incident. Every result or incident has a root cause and most often multiple root causes. If we knew all the incidents that occurred prior to the event, we could more accurately predict the results.

Once we have the forecast, take the necessary actions to insure the results are favorable but consider and be prepared for worst case and consider actions to prevent it.

When results are received, understand the results and why the results happened. Be prepared to adjust your process.

We need to be Boy Scouts and "Be prepared." We need to be chess players and "Think three moves" ahead. Then, if we understand statistical variation and root cause analysis, we are less likely to be surprised.